Trustee Handbook

10TH EDITION

NAIS Trustee Series

Donna Orem and Debra P. Wilson

National Association
of Independent Schools

ISBN: 978-1-63115-003-6
Printed in the United States of America

The National Association of Independent Schools provides services to more than 1,800 schools and associations of schools in the United States and abroad, including 1,500 nonprofit, private K–12 schools in the U.S. that are self-determining in mission and program and are governed by independent boards. NAIS works to empower independent schools and the students they serve.

To find out more information, go to the NAIS website at http://www.nais.org.

Editors: Sarah Hardesty Bray, Susan Hunt, Myra McGovern, and Shannon Spaeder

Designers: Fletcher Design, Inc./Washington, DC (book) and
Kate Purcell Design/Baltimore, MD (cover)

National Association
of Independent Schools

Contents

Foreword

INDEPENDENT SCHOOLS HAVE LONG VALUED great leadership. From the founding of our first schools, visionary leaders have identified needs in their communities, developed strategies to meet those needs, and built support for the schools they established.

As the independent school community evolved from its earliest days, we recognized the value of good governance as a foundation for great leadership. Indeed, independent governance is one of the hallmarks of our industry. Boards of trustees set the context for leadership and establish strategic priorities that will help our schools meet their missions. Trustees are stewards of their schools, ensuring that the school exists not just for today's students but also for future generations.

Today, demographic changes, economic turbulence, growing competition, rapidly emerging new technologies, and other forces are demanding much of independent schools. For many schools, the days of comfortable growth in enrollments and revenues seem well behind us. But these forces also present great opportunities. We need strong, transformative leaders at every level to identify these opportunities and to move our institutions ahead successfully. The school head and board must work together to ask and answer the tough questions. They must cooperate to create a common vision, sometimes looking in new directions.

The current landscape demands changes in how the board does its work and how it collaborates with the head and other top administrators. That is why NAIS is publishing this new version of the *Trustee Handbook*. It underscores and explains the critical new roles that trustees must play if they are to provide the future-focused leadership that our schools need, not just to survive but also to flourish.

The book outlines how to establish clear lines of responsibility, good communication, and a shared commitment to the mission and long-term health of the school, all vital components of good governance. It offers guidance on forming board-head partnerships.

This 10th edition of the *Trustee Handbook* also suggests ways for schools to reduce the time they spend on routine reports and focus instead on the issues of greatest strategic importance to the school. Simply put, the times call for new approaches to trusteeship. According to Richard P. Chait, William P. Ryan, and Barbara E. Taylor in *Governance as Leadership: Reframing the Work of Nonprofit Boards*, the most effective boards operate in three different modes of governance: fiduciary, strategic, and generative. Many boards are familiar with and operate successfully in the first two modes but not the last. In the generative mode, boards take time to assess the broader environment in which their school operates and to discern challenges and opportunities. This mode leads boards to ask questions like, "Are we framing this issue correctly? Are our assumptions correct? What other aspects should we consider?" In the generative mode, the board's central purpose is to be a source of leadership for the institution.

NAIS has, in fact, rethought and reorganized how it does its own work. At meetings, our board now devotes much of its time to generative analysis and discussion. Our trustees are taking on the big questions facing independent schools, such as how to best deal with the proliferation of new competitors, the strengths and weaknesses of the traditional independent school business model, and other issues.

This book describes how boards can manifest the specific qualities of high-performing boards, establishing a strategic orientation and a culture of self-assessment and accountability. It also suggests ways for boards to structure themselves for greater efficiency and innovation.

While the formal authority and oversight rests with the governing board as a whole, each individual member has an impact on a board's overall effectiveness. Every person on the board must be open to new opportunities and new ways of working collaboratively to lead the school. For that reason, this book should be of value to all trustees, whether they are new or experienced board members.

The changes occurring in our society at large and with independent schools in particular call for a significant rethinking of board work in order for our schools to serve our current students and future generations well. Our schools need leaders who can move them forward boldly with courage and insight. This book can help illuminate the path.

Your work on behalf of independent schools and your desire to continually improve the governance and leadership of your own school strengthens our entire community. We appreciate your work as we strive to meet NAIS's mission "to empower independent schools and the students they serve." Thank you.

John Chubb

President
National Association
of Independent Schools

Katherine Dinh

Chair of the NAIS Board of Trustees
Head
Prospect Sierra School (California)

The Independent School Board
Characteristics, Responsibilities, and Qualities

EVERY INDEPENDENT SCHOOL IS DISTINCT, so it's no surprise that the operations and activities of school boards of trustees vary significantly as well. There is no prototypical independent school board; each has its own size, structure, culture, and history, among other things. Yet despite such differences, boards do have several universally accepted responsibilities. And most high-performing boards share certain fundamental characteristics and have similar qualities.

This book will outline those characteristics, responsibilities, and qualities with the goal of educating new trustees and others so they can contribute most effectively to their school's long-term viability and success.

Nonprofit Boards Compared with For-Profit Boards

Independent school boards, like all other boards, are corporate entities with fiduciary duties and an obligation to lead the organization that they oversee toward the fulfillment of its mission and purpose.

However, unlike corporate boards, independent school boards steward institutions that automatically convert any financial gains made in one year into reserves, endowment funds, or additional revenues for the next year's budget. Nonprofit independent school boards also tend to differ from the for-profit corporate model in how they define success, map their way, and interact with their schools.

Although the nonprofit world can be a bit disorienting to trustees who serve on nonprofit boards for the first time, they will find that nonprofit and for-profit boards have similar oversight obligations and fiduciary duties. (For more about fiduciary duties, see Chapter 2.) Those obligations and duties include:

- stewarding the entity toward a long and prosperous future;
- overseeing long- and short-term strategic goals and planning in order to ensure the continuing viability of the entity;
- engaging in matters that guarantee the health of the entity, including risk management, its business model, and its overarching and ongoing financial stability;
- supporting the entity's management as needed; and
- remaining aware of fiduciary obligations to the entity.

Key Characteristics of Independent School Boards

Independent school boards and for-profit boards differ primarily in the terminology they use, their composition, and how they measure success. Trustees on independent school boards will find that the following elements often drive their work:

- **"Trustee" versus "director."** Independent schools tend to have boards of "trustees" as opposed to boards of "directors." While seemingly just a difference in nomenclature — as most states allow the terms "trustee," "director," "member," and others to be used interchangeably — historically, the word "trustee" implies a higher level of discourse, stewardship, and ethical responsibility. This implication comes largely from trust law, whereby trustees hold assets and decisions in care for beneficiaries — much the same way that independent school trustees hold the school in trust for future generations of families. When schools do use the term "director" to refer to their board members, it is usually because a state law issue raises greater obligations under trust law for the board. For example, it is usually due to historic use by the school, a state law issue that requires the use of the term, or a desire to ensure that individuals serving on the board are held to the intended standards under applicable state law.

- **Purpose of the school.** The school's founding documents include its application for nonprofit status filed with the Internal Revenue Service as well as the articles of incorporation. The purpose of the school is often broader than the mission. The purpose is drafted to guide the work of the school but also to provide some degree of flexibility.

- **Mission.** One of the most fundamental differences between a for-profit and nonprofit board is the latter's commitment to mission. While a for-profit entity may have a mission, the nonprofit's mission often defines its key principles and services within its broader purpose. Each school should have a clear mission that sets it apart from other schools, and the board should view that mission as a North Star for guiding its work.

- **Measurement.** A school's mission also drives what the board measures. For-profit boards and investors look to the corporation's financial bottom line to gauge success. In contrast, while the independent school board always wants to make sure that the school is running in a financially stable way, the other key measure of a school is how well it is delivering on its mission — usually a much more amorphous concept.

- **Self-Selection.** Under the various state corporate codes, corporate members — usually shareholders — generally elect for-profit board members. While some nonprofits may have members of a sort, most independent school boards are self-selecting and perpetuating. This process allows boards to identify the skills and perspectives that they will need and to reach out to individuals outside of the immediate community for greater involvement. This approach can significantly strengthen the governance of the school. However, school boards also need to recognize the obligations that result from this level of autonomy.

The independent school board must leverage this self-direction to embrace a broad range of skills and viewpoints as well as to represent the varied interests of the school community rather than creating a board that is largely insular. This self-direction also requires that boards be self-correcting. While for-profit shareholders may vote directors out of office, the same is usually not true for independent school boards. If a board is not leading the school responsibly, the result is often felt in the school itself, causing parents of current students to "vote with their feet" by taking their students out of the school. This trend can be difficult for a school to reverse and can hurt the institution for years to come. For this reason, independent school boards must remain cognizant of the impact of the board's leadership of the school and self-correct — either through future board recruitment or by taking steps to remove board members who may be problematic. Most schools do have a process by which board members may be voted off the board, and responsible boards recognize that, at times, these measures are needed.

- **Membership.** Many people assume that parents fill most of the seats on a school board. However, independent school boards should, and largely do, reflect a broad number of constituencies and perspectives. NAIS strongly recommends that parents make up no more than half of independent school boards, with the other half composed of alumni, former parents, or other interested members of the community. This range of backgrounds and viewpoints helps ensure that the board stays at the strategic level of leadership and focuses on the school's mission and long-term future. It also encourages greater trust in the board among people in the community, as they understand that the board's work extends beyond the day-to-day practices at the school.

Both nonprofit and for-profit boards have similar, long-term fiduciary obligations and a drive to ensure that the corporate entity, whatever it may be, survives and thrives into the future. Nonprofit boards, however, define the long-term success of the institution in a very different way and act as stewards for those whom the school is currently serving and those who will need its services in the future. Everything a board does should support that long-term vision and stewardship ideal in the context of the school's purpose and mission.

Major Responsibilities of Independent School Boards

Mission is paramount at independent schools, and one of the most important responsibilities of every independent school board is to be the guardian of the school's mission. Among other things, the board must adopt the school's mission, vision, and strategic goals and then establish policies and plans that reinforce them.

In addition, each board should be a careful steward of the school's resources and be accountable for the institution's financial stability. Boards oversee operating budgets, ensuring the preservation of capital assets and endowment, and actively help raise money for the school.

Independent school boards must also establish and maintain bylaws that conform to legal requirements — especially their fiduciary duties of loyalty, obedience, and care — as well as always operate in compliance with the law. They must also uphold high ethical standards and avoid conflicts of interest.

Another primary responsibility of the board is to select, hire, evaluate, and establish the compensation of the school head. The board must work in tandem with the head and other school administrators, always being careful to focus its primary work on long-range and strategic issues, not the daily operations of the school.

The board must also keep its own house in order by maintaining accurate records of meetings and policies and ensuring that all its members are actively engaged in board work. It should be open and transparent in terms of communicating its final decisions, yet also keep deliberations confidential. It should develop a clear and intentional program to orient new trustees, continually educate them on the issues before the school, and evaluate their performance. And to guarantee a pipeline of strong leaders, it should put in place a board-leadership succession plan.

Board service requires a significant commitment to the school and its welfare, observance of the highest ethical standards and principles of fiscal integrity, and a readiness to explore challenges and gain consensus with fellow trustees.

For a complete listing of the most important responsibilities of independent school boards, please see NAIS Principles of Good Practice for Boards of Trustees on page 9 and NAIS Principles of Good Practice for Independent School Trustees on page 10.

Top Qualities of High-Performing Independent School Boards

Well-functioning independent school boards establish procedures and processes that help them function efficiently and guide the school in fulfilling what can be an amorphous nonprofit mission. The best-performing boards:

- **understand their role within the school.** The ultimate authority over the school rests with the board, which is responsible for serving the best interests of the school and ensuring its long-term success. At the same time, the board should always avoid straying too deeply into tactical or management decisions. (For more about the role of the board, see Chapter 2.)

- **commit to goals and objectives.** All of the school's goals and objectives should trace back to the mission in some way. These goals should be overarching, with the head of school charged with ensuring that the internal school team is focused on and working toward those goals. Many schools will also have specific board goals in areas such as fund-raising and strategic outreach or other ways of supporting the institution's goals. The school administration and board should revisit these goals every year, generally with an eye toward establishing a handful of larger long-term goals. Many schools have moved beyond creating and following traditional five-year strategic plans, as the environment in which schools now operate is changing too rapidly for detailed strategic plans to remain relevant for long. They are replacing such plans with yearly goal-setting and ongoing strategic thinking. (For more about strategic orientation, see Chapter 3.)

- **use data to inform strategy and track key metrics.** High-performing schools and their boards use data to inform decision-making and measure success. Boards should frequently review the school's overall health through a dashboard of key metrics (e.g., budgeted to actual financial results, the admissions process, alumni giving) and also use data to regularly assess how the school is executing its mission. Such data might include surveys of students, parents, alumni, and staff members, as well as overviews of college or high-school admission trends and the like. The school should also gather assessment data on the board and head of school through annual evaluations and reflection. (For more about using data, see Chapter 3.)

- **focus on ongoing board recruitment.** At independent schools with an effective governance model, continuing assessment of the board's needs through changing goals and objectives, as well as the shifts in the marketplace, is always in progress and evolving. Boards should have an ongoing systematic process of devel-

NAIS PRINCIPLES OF GOOD PRACTICE FOR BOARDS OF TRUSTEES

1. The board adopts a clear statement of the school's mission, vision, and strategic goals and establishes policies and plans consistent with this statement.

2. The board reviews and maintains appropriate bylaws that conform to legal requirements, including duties of loyalty, obedience, and care.

3. The board assures that the school and the board operate in compliance with applicable laws and regulations, minimizing exposure to legal action. The board creates a conflict of interest policy that is reviewed with, and signed by, individual trustees annually.

4. The board accepts accountability for both the financial stability and the financial future of the institution, engaging in strategic financial planning, assuming primary responsibility for the preservation of capital assets and endowments, overseeing operating budgets, and participating actively in fund-raising.

5. The board selects, supports, nurtures, evaluates, and sets appropriate compensation for the head of school.

6. The board recognizes that its primary work and focus are long-range and strategic.

7. The board undertakes formal strategic planning on a periodic basis, sets annual goals related to the plan, and conducts annual written evaluations for the school, the head of school, and the board itself.

8. The board keeps full and accurate records of its meetings, committees, and policies and communicates its decisions widely, while keeping its deliberations confidential.

9. Board composition reflects the strategic expertise, resources, and perspectives (past, present, future) needed to achieve the mission and strategic objectives of the school.

10. The board works to ensure all its members are actively involved in the work of the board and its committees.

11. As leader of the school community, the board engages proactively with the head of school in cultivating and maintaining good relations with school constituents as well as the broader community and exhibits best practices relevant to equity and justice.

12. The board is committed to a program of professional development that includes annual new trustee orientation, ongoing trustee education and evaluation, and board leadership succession planning.

NAIS PRINCIPLES OF GOOD PRACTICE FOR INDEPENDENT SCHOOL TRUSTEES

1. A trustee actively supports and promotes the school's mission, vision, strategic goals, and policy positions.

2. A trustee is knowledgeable about the school's mission and goals, including its commitment to equity and justice, and represents them appropriately and accurately within the community.

3. A trustee stays fully informed about current operations and issues by attending meetings regularly, coming to meetings well prepared, and participating fully in all matters.

4. The board sets policy and focuses on long-range and strategic issues. An individual trustee does not become involved directly in specific management, personnel, or curricular issues.

5. A trustee takes care to separate the interests of the school from the specific needs of a particular child or constituency.

6. A trustee accepts and supports board decisions. Once a decision has been made, the board speaks with one voice.

7. A trustee keeps all board deliberations confidential.

8. A trustee guards against conflict of interest, whether personal or business related.

9. A trustee has the responsibility to support the school and its head and to demonstrate that support within the community.

10. Authority is vested in the board as a whole. A trustee who learns of an issue of importance to the school has the obligation to bring it to the head of school, or to the board chair, and must refrain from responding to the situation individually.

11. A trustee contributes to the development program of the school, including strategic planning for development, financial support, and active involvement in annual and capital giving.

12. Each trustee, not just the treasurer and finance committee, has fiduciary responsibility to the school for sound financial management.

oping a pipeline of talent for the board. (For more about board recruitment, see Chapter 4.)

- **plan carefully for leadership succession.** A strong board is always assessing its leadership needs and ensuring that it has a written board-leadership succession strategy. As part of that, the board must clearly identify a core number of leadership positions and design a leadership succession process that is confidential but also guided by principles of openness and inclusivity. The board should also regularly assess the performance of people in leadership roles. (For more about leadership succession, see Chapter 4.)

- **engage in continuing professional development and education.** Board members often have full-time jobs and are usually not immersed in the independent school world. They should engage in educational opportunities ranging from basic orientation for new trustees to training on the independent school financial model to overviews of community demographics. Also, before a board takes on a particular challenge, it should receive — through overviews from staff members, reports on data trends, or other insights — additional education to help inform any of its decisions. Trustees must make time for all of these trainings and opportunities to ensure effective leadership. In addition, they should make an effort to get to know each other better so that they can work effectively as a team. (For more about board development, see Chapter 5.)

- **regularly assess their performance.** Such assessments help the board advance the school's long-term objectives, remind board members of their responsibilities and increase their accountability, and create a stronger board team. Some of the areas that can be assessed include the board's work in supporting the institution's mission and the board's working relationships with the school head and other senior administrators. (For more about board self-assessment, see Chapter 5.)

- **structure themselves for efficiency and innovation.** Boards should keep a close eye on how they are structured and operate. They should have a firm grasp on what processes help or hinder their efforts on behalf of the school. Today, many school boards are changing how they organize themselves so as to promote a more strategic approach. (For more about board structure, see Chapter 6.)

- **understand their school's financial model and current trends in independent school education.** Boards today are helping their institutions develop more stable financial structures by exploring new partnerships, creating auxiliary businesses, and using technology to cut costs, among other strategies. They are also knowledgeable about the education landscape and the context in which their school must operate. (For more about the changing landscape in education, see Chapter 7.)

- **establish and follow a clear agenda.** Boards should have a firm grasp of when key decisions must be made throughout the year and map those needs on a formal board calendar. Budget building, evaluations, goal-setting, and similar activities usually occur at the same time every year, and these items should receive appropriate room on that calendar. Boards should also schedule in the calendar the strategic questions for each board meeting to align with the goals and objectives for that year and the longer-term goals of the school. (For a sample calendar of board meetings, see Appendix A.)

In the pages that follow, we will provide greater detail on each of these and other qualities of top-performing boards, especially in the independent school context. We hope these standards and ideals will inform independent school board members of their obligations and inspire them to contribute as effectively as possible to the institutions they serve.

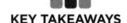

KEY TAKEAWAYS

- While nomenclature and processes may differ, both nonprofit and for-profit boards are responsible for stewarding the entity toward a long and prosperous future.

- The school's purpose and mission are the overarching principles that guide the work of both the board and the school's leadership.

- Data and context inform the work of the board and school leadership as they lead the school in fulfillment of its purpose and mission.

- The school must find a way to measure its definition of success (beyond just financial measures) in relation to the school's purpose and mission.

- Board and school processes and procedures should support the school's quest to fulfill its mission. These processes and procedures must include goal and objective setting; board education; regular evaluation of the school's progress toward its goals; and an organized, thoughtful way of leading the school to accomplish these goals.

2

A Shared Understanding of Roles and Responsibilities

FOR AN INDEPENDENT SCHOOL to work efficiently and effectively, all of its leaders must have a clear understanding of the functions and responsibilities they must perform. And the functions and responsibilities of trustees can be among the most complex.

Trustees rarely play just one role within a school. They are often parents, parents of alumni, major donors, interested community members, and/or grandparents. Each of these outside roles can impact how a trustee serves the school. Indeed, the personal interests that often inspire someone to want to become a trustee can create the greatest confusion in his or her understanding of the position.

Beyond this complexity of multiple roles, trustees are also the alter ego of the school. They represent its governing body, overseeing the long-term course of the institution and responsible to the federal and state government for the school's lawful operation in pursuit of its mission. As such, the board is the most influential group within the school. Therefore, trustees must understand the obligations of their governance role and responsibly serve in that capacity to ensure the healthy functioning of the school.

Job Description

Some trustees want a basic list of all of the things they need to "do." Such a written job description for trustees can be difficult to draft. Trustees are expected to oversee, lead, know, understand, and be ultimately responsible for the school — all without overly interfering with the school's operations or quitting their day jobs. Yet gray areas and overlaps between trustee oversight and the daily administration of the school can develop in a number of situations. Many boards have trustee job descriptions to help clarify these expectations and guide board members in their work. Those written descriptions can be helpful in laying out what's expected of the individual board members, particularly when a school has specific expectations. (For sample language related to duties of board leaders, see Appendix B.) A board manual can also clarify expectations. (For sample contents of a board manual, see Appendix C.)

With or without a written job description, trustees must gain an understanding of the key responsibilities that drive their work, as well as some of the limitations on that work. Whether schools use job descriptions or not, they should be clear and deliberate in the expectations of board members, in terms of both duties and behaviors. These expectations are often outlined in the school's board policies.

In addition, all trustees are bound by the basic fiduciary obligations found in each state, and many of those obligations are hallmarks of good trusteeship. Such obligations include coming to meetings, remaining informed, putting the school first in the person's dealings, and the like. This chapter will outline some of those obligations in detail and provide some guiding principles to help trustees understand what will be required of them in serving on almost any independent school board.

Trustee "Hats"

Trustees must fulfill their responsibilities with an overarching awareness of the specific roles they play within independent schools. Above all, a trustee must understand the *primacy* of his or her role relative to any other connection he or she may have with the school. Trustees are responsible for serving in the best interest of the school, and to do that well, they must learn to put aside their daily interactions with the school and keep an eye on the larger picture. For a current parent, this means not using the position to influence the school in any way for oneself or one's children. For an alum, this means broadening the lens beyond one's own school experience.

Keeping roles distinct can be particularly difficult if the board includes people who serve ex officio on it, such as the president of the parents' association or the alumni association. Although these individuals may automatically serve on the board by virtue of their roles in these capacities, they need to understand that *on the board*, they do not represent these groups. They should also understand that they are bound by confidentiality and other policies if they report back to these community groups in any way.

Another important element for trustees to understand is that no one individual has power beyond the whole board. The power of the board is with the collective body. In this way, no individual board member — including the board chair — is more powerful than any other. What can complicate matters is that the wider community often does not understand that individual board members, particularly the officers, do not automatically have wider authority. For this reason, it is imperative that the board speak with one consistent voice, even if individual board members do not agree on the final, board-ratified decision or direction. When board members attempt to act individually, or to speak on behalf of the board or a portion of the board when there has been no such empowerment, community confusion almost always ensues. The only time a board member may have greater individual authority is when specific powers, such as check-writing ability, are assigned to a certain position on the board. Even then, the school should have checks and balances built into such power.

The Trustee's Role Versus the Staff's Role

The board is charged with overseeing the head of school and the overall, long-term strategic and fiscal viability of the institution. To maintain this higher-level oversight, the board must stay out of the day-to-day work of the head and staff. This can be particularly challenging in smaller schools where boards may feel that they should take a more active role.

Such issues tend to present themselves in a few different areas, such as the following:

- **Communicating input from a community member.** If a trustee receives feedback or insight from a student, parent, alumni, staff member, or other person in the school community, he or she should bring that information to the wider board through either the head of school or the board chair. These communication systems ensure that the board consistently represents the community as a whole and can respond thoughtfully and cogently to any specific concerns. This approach also gives the board a holistic view of feedback from the community.

- **Striking the proper level of discourse during meetings.** When the board or a board committee discusses a school issue, it should avoid straying too deeply into tactical or management decisions reserved for the school staff. All board members have an obligation to direct the conversation back to a more strategic level if the board begins to wander into such areas.

- **Handling concerns of school management.** Occasionally, school leaders will either inform the board of a day-to-day school concern or request guidance from the board on a tactical issue that has a broad public relations impact. Such conversations must be handled with the utmost care to respect the board's obligation to the bigger picture and overall risk management of the school, as well as the administration's responsibility to deal with these matters directly. An example of such an incident is when a longtime employee is consistently not performing up to expectations and has not responded to improvement plans, but the school administration knows that letting this employee go will cause significant upheaval among alumni and current families. The school leadership team does not want the board to be surprised by such an action and may want input from the board — or an individual trustee or board committee — on how the situation should be handled.

The Fiduciary Obligations of Trustees

Like all board members of for-profit and nonprofit entities, independent school trustees have certain fiduciary responsibilities. While they vary slightly from state to state, the fundamental legal obligations are generally considered to be: (1) the duty of care, (2) the duty of loyalty, and (3) the duty of obedience.

Duty of Care

The duty of care requires trustees to take the requisite care in their work for their institution. State laws largely mandate that such care be "reasonable." To fulfill this duty, trustees must be reasonably informed, participate in decisions, and do so in good faith and with the care of an ordinarily prudent person in similar circumstances.

Boards address this particular duty in the following ways:

- **Proper board development.** Boards should identify and recruit the most appropriate new members, clearly communicate the expectations of board service to them, and provide them with orientation and ongoing training.

- **A focus on purpose and mission.** Every action that a board takes should be made with the school's corporate purpose and mission in mind.

- **Confidentiality.** Trustees must keep board deliberations, decisions, and school information absolutely confidential. Trustees are entrusted with competitively sensitive information, as well as confidential information relating to employees and, occasionally, community members. Trustees must not share this information with anyone else, including spouses, friends, or other school community members.

- **Stewardship of resources.** Trustees should ensure, to a reasonable degree, that the school's resources are sufficient for its undertaking, are used rationally in the school's projects, and are otherwise protected from being wasted or misappropriated. Boards do this through the budgeting and audit processes, as well as through strategic controls.

- **Attendance at meetings.** A board should have a policy that encourages members to attend meetings. Many school bylaws include terms that allow for the automatic resignation of a board member after he or she misses a set number of meetings in a row. Other schools have a less formal policy, one that simply requires the chair of the governance committee or the board chair to follow up personally with board members who consistently fail to attend the meetings. Either way, attendance is a crucial aspect of this fiduciary obligation.

- **Preparation and engagement.** Board members must read in advance any materials they receive before meetings and then actively participate in the meetings they attend. Active participation may include asking hard questions about proposed plans or approaches and requesting additional information about them. Trustees are expected to exercise this kind of due diligence in fulfilling their duties.

- **Prudent delegation of authority.** A trustee's duty of care cannot be transferred to anyone else. He or she should not, for example, send a business associate to attend a board meeting because of a scheduling conflict, and the board should not permit such a delegate to sit. A trustee may rely on professional opinion and counsel from accountants, attorneys, executive compensation analysts, investment advisors, and the like as long as he or she has no reason to question the expertise or independence of the person giving the advice. Similarly, a trustee may rely on the advice and conclusions of a committee of the board of which the trustee is not a member. But the trustee should do so only if he or she is confident that the committee is knowledgeable about the matter in question and that no member of the committee has any apparent conflict of interest regarding it.

- **Oversight of the head of school.** A crucial element of the duty of care is the oversight of the head of school. The board must walk a careful balance here, as nonprofit boards tend to give great deference to the CEO. However, it is always the duty of

---

CONFLICTS OF INTEREST

The duty of loyalty is embodied in conflict-of-interest policies and procedures. These policies and procedures provide mechanisms for trustees to raise or acknowledge potential conflicts — those situations where a trustee's personal interest may be an issue in the school's dealings — as well as to manage those conflicts. Often such policies require yearly signed statements from trustees as well as an ongoing awareness during the year as issues unfold.

Disclosure, tracking, and the proper handling of conflicts of interest are vital for nonprofits like independent schools because so much of these institutions' success depends on the public trust that they build with their communities. A hint of self-dealing can be devastating to any nonprofit, but particularly for a school, which is entrusted with the academic and moral education of children. Further, by virtue of being a nonprofit, a school is required not to serve the interests of any one individual, and self-dealing can cause that status to be legally revoked.

the board and individual trustees to scrutinize whether the head is carrying out the purpose and mission of the school, as well as the policies and direction that the board has established, and otherwise acting in the best interests of the institution. This oversight includes setting reasonable compensation and benefits for the school head and being knowledgeable about that compensation package.

Duty of Loyalty

The duty of loyalty requires that a trustee always act in the best interests of the institution without regard to his or her personal interest or that of any other individual. This includes not taking an opportunity available to the school and personally exploiting it. It does not mean that someone should automatically be disqualified from serving as a trustee because an act that the school might take one day could affect his or her personal interest (for example, parents on a board who vote for tuition increases). Rather, it means that if such a situation arises, the board and individual trustees should take all reasonable measures to manage the conflict of interest to the benefit of the school. (See the sidebar on page 22. For a sample Conflict-of-Interest Statement, see Appendix N.)

For additional guidance and examples, see the NAIS publication *Holding the Trust: An Independent School Trustee's Guide to Fiduciary Responsibilities*.

Duty of Obedience

The duty of obedience requires that the board and individual trustees remain faithful to the purpose and mission of the school. The governing documents, such as the articles of incorporation and the bylaws, set forth the purpose of the school, while the mission statement articulates its mission. As part of fulfilling the duty of obedience, the board should keep in mind:

- **The use of resources.** The board should ensure that the school uses its resources appropriately and well, including donations given for a particular purpose.

- **Compliance with the law.** The duty of obedience also requires that the school operate within the law, including nonprofit, employment, and other laws. While it is certainly not possible for trustees to guarantee compliance with all laws in all respects, nor is it expected that they do so, the board should establish procedures by which trustees can monitor whether the school's administration is being attentive to its legal obligations.

Developing and Reviewing Board Policies

Boards develop and review institutional policies for their schools to provide overall guidance in particular areas of importance to both school leadership and the broader school community. Policy oversight and development can be one of the trickier places for the board to keep its finger on the pulse of the school, as these policies reflect both the heart of the school's culture and intention as well as risk management for the institution. Moreover, not all policies are board policies to be implemented. The administration carries out operational and procedural policies pursuant to the board policies.

For example, a board may have an overarching institutional policy on the many facets of diversity, its importance to the school, and the need for the school to reflect the diversity of the wider world.

Design of the Board-Head Partnership: Time and Attention

Policies **Strategies** Mission Survival Leadership	**BOARD'S DECISIONS** Head's Advice
Partnership Authorizations Finance policies Enrollment Employment terms	**SHARED DECISIONS: BOARD AND HEAD**
Operational Admissions Staffing Program Systems	Board's Advice **HEAD'S DECISIONS**

This chart shows the appropriate allocation of the board's and the head's time.

This policy may then inform the admissions and financial aid policies and procedures that the school's administration implements. (For a checklist of policies and a risk management checklist, see Appendices D and E.)

In this way, institutional policies provide the board a way to guide, inform, or focus the work of the school without crossing into operational or management territory. This is one area where the various roles of board members and staff members can become complicated and tend to overlap, as the head of school or administrative team is often helpful in drafting, informing, or partnering with the board on institutional policies. However, the board should not serve in a similar capacity in the administration's development of the related operational or procedural policies.

When boards look at overall institutional policies, they should bear in mind not only the policies that reflect the culture and mission of the school but also the risk management areas that should be addressed. The board should be aware of major areas that deserve policy coverage and ensure that responsive policies exist and are current and readily accessible to those who will be affected by them. As a follow-up, the board must work with school leaders to ensure that they draft and implement appropriate procedural and operational policies. The board might well ask for periodic reports on the application of major new policies. (A regular long-term plan should schedule one or more policy areas for board review each year.) In its book *Effective Governing Boards*, the Association of Governing Boards of Universities and Colleges (AGB) provides questions for boards to ask, including the following:

- Which policies and procedures require board approval and which should be adopted and promulgated by the administration?
- What is the role of the institution's legal counsel in reviewing and approving proposed new or revised policies and ensuring their compatibility with the charter, bylaws, and institutional mission?
- Is there a schedule for periodic board review of major policy areas?
- What is the protocol for assigning responsibility for initiating such reviews, identifying policy gaps, and recommending policy additions and changes?[1]

Cultivating Philanthropy

Philanthropy is a fundamental part of the successful financial operation of an independent school. As stewards of the school's financial success, trustees must diligently oversee the multiple aspects of this area. To do so, trustees should look at philanthropy in the school holistically. The advancement work in the school is not just about giving money to the school on a regular basis; it is much more than that. The relative success of the advancement work will be based on the breadth and depth of the philanthropic culture within the school. The board leads this culture by individually and collectively participating in the annual fund or capital campaign, as well as being visible throughout the school's fund-raising work.

As fund-raising is a fundamental part of virtually every school's operating budget, trustees' first obligation is to ensure that the advancement work is well resourced for success and has the appropriate attention of the staff and the board. Reasonable goals that appropriately address the needs of the school and its budget should be in place, with the objectives to help achieve those goals.

Virtually all schools have a board committee specifically focused on advancement work. This committee helps build the various goals and objectives of the board and other constituents in this area, works with those various constituencies, and tracks fund-raising progress throughout the school year. While the committee serves as the lead for board engagement on this topic, other board members must remain involved and ready to help.

Trustees should also financially support the school's fund-raising efforts. All independent school trustees are expected to participate in fund-raising activities and to make their independent school a primary charity to which they contribute. About 50 percent of independent school boards require that trustees make some form of monetary contribution to the school.[2]

Beyond personal giving, schools generally expect trustees to be representatives to the outside world and to help them in their fund-raising efforts as needed. For additional guidance, see NAIS's publication *The Trustee's Role in Fund-Raising.*

While each school's advancement office will guide its trustees' involvement, generally that involvement includes being present for particular school events, hosting events either at home or elsewhere, helping make contacts within the community, or helping solicit funds for the school. Independent schools work with their trustees to ensure that they are comfortable with participation in advancement work.

A Final Word on a Shared Understanding of Roles and Responsibilities

Being a trustee at an independent school can be a messy business. While the basic fiduciary obligations and requirements of board policies and procedures are often quite clear, the actual work — usually done closely with the head of school and administrative team — can be complicated by the tensions between strategic leadership from the board and the operational and management activities of the administration. The two do not happen in a vacuum and often will overlap.

When boards and administrations find themselves in these gray areas, they do best to operate from a position of trust and camaraderie and openly discuss the issues they are facing. Trust within the board and between the board and the school leadership are fundamental to properly tackling these potential quagmires.

ENDNOTES

[1] Association of Governing Board of Universities and Colleges, *A Guide for Members of Governing Boards of Independent Colleges and Universities* (Washington, DC: 2009).

[2] NAIS, *Heads and Boards Working in Partnership: 2012–13 NAIS Governance Study* (Washington, DC: 2013); available in the NAIS bookstore at http://www.nais.org/bookstore.

KEY TAKEAWAYS

- Trustees may be aware of their job descriptions, but they should also always bear in mind the wider obligations required of them.

- The board should perform its work from the perspective of a reasonable person whose only interest in the school is its long-term success and the stewardship of it for current and future generations. Trustees should be prepared to check their other hats at the door.

- Because board work will almost always involve the head of school or administrative team, crossover into the gray space between the board's leadership and that of the administrative team is almost impossible to avoid. When it happens, a culture and climate of trust and openness between both is essential to successful leadership and the attainment of goals.

- Board policies help the board provide concrete, mission-related direction to the operational policies and approaches that the school takes without inviting the board into the school management processes.

- Fund-raising is a fundamental piece of being a board member, through both personal giving and aiding the advancement office in its efforts to raise funds and awareness within the community.

3

A Strong Strategic Orientation

EVERY INDEPENDENT SCHOOL BOARD adopts a certain way of operating — either by designation, leadership, or a culture that has formed over time. This modus operandi is usually ingrained in the board, and significant change occurs only when some event or leader comes around to disrupt the way the board functions. But to be effective, boards need to be intentional in their goals, their roles, and the impact they want to have on the school that they lead. Put simply, they must have a strong sense of purpose.

Three Levels of Governance

One of the most important guides to successful board governance is *Governance as Leadership: Reframing the Work of Nonprofit Boards* by Richard Chait, William Ryan, and Barbara Taylor. This research-based work lays out an excellent framework to help boards gain that sense of purpose and be the best stewards of their institutions over both the short and the long term.

The book describes the most effective boards as operating in three different modes of governance. The following provides general summaries of the modes:[1]

- **The Fiduciary Mode.** In this mode, probably the best known and understood by trustees, the board oversees operations and ensures efficient and appropriate use of resources, legal compliance, and fiscal accountability. This is important work, as it makes certain that the school is solvent and stays out of legal troubles. But operating in this mode alone does not provide the kind of governance leadership that a school needs.

- **The Strategic Mode.** Most trustees are aware of the need to operate in the strategic mode when engaged in strategic planning, but what does it mean to be strategic in continuing operations? In this mode, the board, in partnership with the head of school, sets the ongoing strategy for the school and measures performance against plans. Being informed by data is very important when operating in the strategic mode. Later in this chapter, we'll discuss the kind of data that trustees should be reviewing on a regular basis.

- **The Generative Mode.** Most board members are probably the least familiar with this mode. When the board is functioning at this level, it is taking the time to make sense of the circumstances and broader environment in which the school operates. In this mode, the board's central purpose is to be a source of leadership for the institution, to discern challenges and opportunities, and to probe assumptions.

Effective boards understand the importance of operating in all three modes, but it can be tricky to put this approach into practice.

Modes of Governance

	Type I **Fiduciary**	Type II **Strategic**	Type III **Generative**
Nature of organizations	Bureaucratic	Open system	Nonrational
Nature of leadership	Hierarchical	Analytical/ visionary	Reflective learners
Board's central purpose	Stewardship of tangible assets	Strategic partnership with management	Source of leadership for organization
Board's core work	Technical: oversee operations, ensure accountability	Analytical: shape strategy, review performance	Creative: discern problems, engage in sense making
Board's principal role	Sentinel	Strategist	Sense maker
Key question	What's wrong?	What's the plan?	What's the question?
Problems are to be	Spotted	Solved	Framed
Deliberative process	Parliamentary and orderly	Empirical and logical	Robust and sometimes playful
Way of deciding	Reaching resolution	Reaching consensus	Grappling and grasping
Way of knowing	It stands to reason	The pieces all fit	It makes sense
Communication with constituents	Limited, ritualized to legitimate	Bilateral, episodic to advocate	Multilateral, ongoing to learn
Performance metrics	Facts, figures, finances, reports	Strategic indicators, competitive analysis	Signs of learning and discerning

Source: Chait, Ryan, and Taylor, *Governance as Leadership: Reframing the Work of Nonprofit Boards*

Using Data to Inform Strategy

In order to function in all modes effectively, boards should build into their operations the practice of collecting and analyzing data and research. The first step is to identify the kind of information a board needs, how often it needs it, and who will collect it. NAIS already makes much of this data readily available, and a school's top administrators and individual trustees can easily access it. NAIS recommends that every school board, working in concert with the head and school leadership team, establish a research agenda as in the example on pages 36–37.

Other types of research can also be beneficial in providing insights to drive strategic decisions, such as *faculty/staff needs and satisfaction research* (to inform decisions about salaries and benefits, alert the school to possible attrition that could affect its performance, or provide a window into what is driving school culture, both negatively and positively) and *student engagement research* (to provide insights into how students are engaged or disengaged). The school can also pinpoint areas of weakness and strength within itself by comparing the results of a student engagement survey with those of a young alumni survey.

The bottom line is that data and research are essential tools for boards to use in making informed strategic decisions. Without accurate data and research, boards can focus resources on the wrong things or spin their wheels by trying to move in too many directions simultaneously.

Scanning the Environment

Boards that excel in both the strategic and generative modes also engage in periodic environmental scanning to uncover trends that may affect the health and well-being of their schools or offer new opportunities for growth and development. Environmental scanning involves following these types of trends:

- Economic (changes in the local market, such as employment and housing prices)
- Legal and political (new legislation or regulations that could impact schools)
- Regional (important themes affecting the entire area)
- Technological (new technological advancements)
- Population (demographic changes)
- Competition (new entrants into a school market)
- Social (such as consumer trends and shifting parent attitudes)

Boards that regularly scan the environment can keep their schools ahead of negative incidents and trends or help them be the first to jump on new opportunities. Scanning is particularly important for the generative mode as it allows boards to make sense of changes in the world in which their institutions operate. In fact, some boards have established a committee with the specific responsibility to scan the environment continually and engage the entire board in discussions around those trends that are most likely to provide opportunities or challenges.

Shared Governance

The most effective boards build a foundation in which all three modes of operation can flourish. This foundation consists of trust and shared leadership.

Establishing a Research Agenda

Type of Data	Why It Is Important	How Often to Conduct
Demographic Data	Reviewing demographic data regularly can provide a road map to how a school's recruitment market is changing over time. Viewing these data can help the board and school leaders forecast when a school might face enrollment challenges and enable them to strategize in advance to cope with those challenges. NAIS's online Demographic Center (available at http://www.nais.org) supplies information on all aspects of the school-age population, which can be analyzed by a variety of geographic filters: counties, zip codes, block groups, and so on.	Annually
Alumni Data	Conducting and analyzing alumni research can help a board understand how well the school is delivering on its mission, how connected its alums feel to the school today, and whether alums will support the school as it launches a fund-raising campaign. Young alumni surveys can be particularly helpful in assessing how well the school is preparing its alums for their next level of education. NAIS offers alumni survey templates through its Survey Center (available at http://www.nais.org).	Every few years

Type of Data	Why It Is Important	How Often to Conduct
Parent Research	Parent satisfaction surveys can help the board stay apprised of what aspects of the school program parents perceive as working well and where they see challenges. In addition, surveying parents whose children were admitted to the school but declined to attend can provide insights into the decision-making factors that led them to choose another institution. NAIS offers parent survey templates through its Survey Center (available at http://www.nais.org).	Every few years
Image/Brand Value Assessment	Studies of how the recruiting market views the institution in relation to other schools can help pinpoint why the school is losing students or what aspects of its program must be enhanced in order to increase market share. Brand assessments also can signal a change in what the market values or the arrival of new competition. These kinds of studies can be particularly helpful when conducted before the beginning of a strategic planning process. NAIS has a research partner that offers a brand assessment (more information is available through Rockbridge Associates at http://www.rockresearch.com/nais-school-study/, or a school can hire a market research firm to conduct a study.	Every five years

Trust is extremely important in the relationship between the school head and the board, and both sides of this partnership need to work to nurture it. A trustee can pursue many approaches that contribute to the growth and development of this partnership:

- **Respect.** Even though board members can (and should) differ in their opinions, they should each respect those differences. It is healthy for board members to disagree with each other and the head, but this must happen in an atmosphere of mutual respect.

- **Transparency.** The school head and the board must be open and transparent with their words and actions. The boardroom should be a place where all opinions can be expressed and heard. All trustees should resist having the "meeting after the meeting."

- **Rule of "No Surprises."** Particularly in the head-board relationship, it is important to subscribe to the rule of no surprises, which simply means sharing all pertinent information.

- **Communication.** Effective boards understand that communication is central to trust. Boards should ensure that effective communication loops are built between the board and the school head, among the committees, and between the board and the local community.

Boards can also best nurture strategic and generative modes of operating in an atmosphere of shared leadership. In *Governance as Leadership*, Chait, Ryan, and Taylor outline four different styles of board operations: (1) Governance by default: Neither the board nor the head of school plays a strong, forward-thinking role; (2) Governance by fiat: The board imposes most decisions; (3) Executive governance: The head governs, and the board is mostly passive; and (4) Shared governance: Both the head and the board are actively engaged in governance.[2]

All boards should take stock and be honest with themselves about which of the four modes best depicts their current style of operation. Only boards that have truly moved to shared governance will function well in the strategic and generative modes. If boards are not operating in the style of shared governance, then they should discuss the path to getting there and set performance goals to ensure that they are successfully working toward it.

Some trustees may ask whether a board can function well in these other styles without strong shared governance. Certainly, some aspects of governance may be accomplished when shared governance is not the norm, but without it boards and their institutions usually encounter many risks and lost opportunities. Chait and his co-authors describe the following outcomes of not embracing shared governance:

- The board functions well only in committees.
- Board members become disengaged.
- There is a lack of strategic thinking.
- The board becomes polarized.
- School boards that remain in the status quo can miss out on growth opportunities for the school.[3]

In *Shared Governance in Times of Change*, Steven C. Bahls, president of Augustana College, outlines a number of ways that shared governance can enable board members and top administrators to make better informed and timely decisions, respond to new demands, and position themselves for the future. Here are some of the aspects of shared governance that he cites:

- **A shared understanding of the deep consequences of transformative change.** To deal with change and plan effectively, trustees and administrators must agree on the challenges they face.

- **A shared sense of urgency.** By recognizing together that the challenges will not simply go away in time, they will be able to take the bold strategic steps needed for success.

- **A shared commitment to do strategic planning and implement plans in a timely and sustained way.** The institution can flourish over the long run when the board and administration collaborate to respond in a strategic, rather than an ad hoc, manner to institutional challenges.

- **A deep pool of trust, understanding, and goodwill.** The benefits include a faster, more effective implementation of ideas, mutual investment in the outcomes, and a sense of shared purpose — in short, a way of working collaboratively toward a common vision.[4]

Finally, a key means of encouraging a board to operate with a strategic orientation is through ongoing board education and development. This begins with a formal trustee orientation, includes continuing board education, and requires periodic self-assessments. We will discuss these in greater detail in Chapter 5.

ENDNOTES

[1] Richard P. Chait, William P. Ryan, and Barbara E. Taylor, *Governance as Leadership: Reframing the Work of Nonprofit Boards* (Washington, DC: BoardSource, 2004).

[2] Ibid.

[3] Ibid.

[4] Steven C. Bahls, *Shared Governance in Times of Change: A Practical Guide for Universities and Colleges* (Washington, DC: Association of Governing Boards of Universities and Colleges, 2014).

KEY TAKEAWAYS

- To govern effectively, boards need to operate in three different modes: fiduciary, strategic, and generative.

- To function productively in the strategic and generative modes, boards should build ongoing processes for data collection and analysis. The most successful boards use data and research to inform strategic decisions.

- Environmental scanning is an essential tool for boards to keep abreast of trends that may be affecting the school and to make sense of circumstances.

- Respect, trust, transparency, and communication are the foundations of a healthy board.

- Shared governance is essential to operating in all three modes.

A Solid System for Building the Board

BOARD SUCCESSION PLANNING is one of the most important responsibilities of an independent school board. Too often, the recruitment and selection of new trustees, and the identification of board officers, happen just once a year, rather than as part of an ongoing systematic process of developing a pipeline of talent for the board. Yet boards that establish formal succession processes find that they are well-equipped to serve their schools, have fewer issues with continuity of leadership, and lead with a more strategic orientation.

The process of developing a board talent pipeline should begin with a vision. As the Cheshire Cat said to Alice in *Through the Looking Glass*, "If you don't know where you're going, any road will get you there." Being clear about the long-term vision for the school helps the board determine the kinds of leadership traits, skills, and abilities it will need to guide the school toward that vision. Although the governance or trustee committee takes the lead in this process, every board member plays a role, beginning with the identification of potential trustees.

Identifying Potential Trustees

When looking for new members, boards should explore a number of obvious, and not so obvious, groups and organizations to identify potential trustees:

- **Current trustees.** Because of their knowledge of the school and its mission and vision, current trustees can be particularly helpful in finding potential ones. Candidates can come from the networks they have within the school, professional colleagues, or acquaintances in the community. Every trustee should see the identification and cultivation of new members as a required responsibility of serving on the board.

- **Volunteers to the school.** Being passionate about the school is an essential trait for any board member, so looking at those people who have already shown their commitment by volunteering is a great way to spot new board talent. This group could include parents, grandparents, alumni, and alumni parents — all of whom can make excellent trustees.

- **Donors.** Giving money to the school is another way that people demonstrate commitment, and those people who have donated over a significant period can be good trustee candidates. At the same time, however, boards should be wary of building a board that is too slanted toward fund-raising. The best boards are diverse in every way and include people who can make all kinds of contributions, not just financial ones.

- **Educational leaders from other schools and organizations.** It is always a good practice to have outside educational experts on the board. Trustees who have this background can add context to school-based discussions and offer a perspective on how the larger educational community views the school. In a *Harvard Business Review* article on nonprofit boards, Taylor, Chait, and Holland note, "Expert trustees can guide fellow board members through a foreign culture."[1] Such trustees can be heads, assistant heads, or division heads from non-competing schools; administrative leaders; or teachers. For example, an educational leader from a school that provides students to the school, often called a "feeder" school, can be a good source of recruitment insight or a strong board member himself or herself.

- **Professionals in the community.** Many types of professionals in the community can serve as effective trustees, but they are often overlooked because they have no personal connection to the school. It is precisely because they have little knowledge of the school that they can be valuable board members. They can see issues with new eyes and provide insights that people closer to the school cannot. Lawyers, doctors, therapists, religious leaders, bankers, entrepreneurs, and others in the community can be potential candidates.

- **Members of other nonprofit boards.** Individuals who serve on other types of nonprofit boards can be good candidates for independent school boards. Board members can identify potential trustees by looking at boards of nonprofits with missions that are synergistic in some way with that of the school.

- **Organizations representing racial/ethnic groups.** Minority groups in the community can also be good sources of potential trustees. People from these types of organizations can offer new perspectives around diversity issues and shine a light on how the board can be more inclusive in its practices.

- **Board training organizations.** Some local communities are home to organizations that train people to serve on nonprofit boards. The board should research whether any such groups are operating in its region, as they will most likely be able to help identify potential trustees.

Diversifying Boards

Most effective boards are diverse in virtually every way — gender, age, race/ethnicity, religion, background, resources, opinions — the list goes on. According to BoardSource, an organization serving nonprofit boards, "Homogeneous boards can result in near-sightedness and group-think, while boards composed of individuals with a variety of skills, perspectives, backgrounds, and resources promote creativity and innovation."[2] In addition, for independent schools seeking to recruit a diverse workforce and student body, embracing diverse governance can be key to success in these arenas.

To build a diverse board, however, one has to lay the groundwork. In the ninth edition of NAIS's *Trustee Handbook*, author Mary DeKuyper suggests a number of steps:

- Be sure the board chair, head, and chair of the committee on trustees or governance agree that having a diverse board is critical to the board's effectiveness and that they will exercise strong leadership on this issue.

- Hold a board conversation, and ask questions such as "Does our board composition reflect the community we serve?"

- Develop a plan for change.[3]

When a board seeks to add members who are not affiliated with the school in any way, it must take similar steps to ensure that it is open to outside views. If the board is not yet ready to accept these outside voices, new trustees can feel isolated and their opinions discounted. This can create factions within the board that foster ineffective governance.

Cultivating Trustees

Once the board identifies a pipeline of potential trustees, it must cultivate those people and establish a connection to its work and the school in general. Current board members can accomplish this in several ways:

- **Ongoing communications.** Working with school staff, board members can create a routine communique informing potential trustees of key happenings at the school and any strategic plans underway.

- **School events.** Current board members who are assigned potential members can invite them to school events and introduce them to other trustees and school leaders.

- **One-on-one meetings.** Current board members can also take candidates out for coffee to answer questions about the school or how the board works.

- **Task forces and committees.** The board can ask potential trustees to serve on task forces or committees that take best advantage of their skills and abilities.

The board should keep potential trustees involved in the work and life of the school in the same way that fund-raisers cultivate potential donors.

Ensuring the Fit

Before the board even begins to consider a slate of possible trustees, it must ensure that each candidate is a good fit for its needs and
culture and will contribute to the growth and development of the
school. Too often board members are chosen simply because they
are major donors to the school or their current role fills an identified
board need. Boards should take not only these considerations into
account but also many others before inviting someone to serve on
the board.

In an interview, Kay Sprinkel Grace, author of *The Ultimate
Board Member's Book*, suggests that one of the most important criteria for selecting a trustee is that he or she cares deeply about the mission of the organization.[4] Without this emotional connection, it may
be hard to get the kind of commitment needed. Here are some other
questions to consider before asking a person to serve on the board:

- Will this person fulfill an important need of the board?
- Does he or she have a basic understanding of the school and its mission?
- Can this person commit to coming to board meetings and giving the time needed to be an effective board member?
- Does he or she have an understanding of a trustee's roles and responsibilities?
- Does this person understand that, as a trustee, he or she will not be representing a specific group or constituency?
- Is this person prepared to make the school a giving priority during his or her service on the board?

In addition, a great way for boards to discover how prospective trustees think and approach challenges is to ask them for their views on leadership or discuss with them some of the issues facing the school.

Ideally, most if not all candidates for the board should be invited to first serve on a committee or task force. This is the best method for discovering how they will perform as a member of a group, how committed they are to doing what is asked of them (reading committee reports, coming to meetings prepared, and the like), and how they will approach the challenges and opportunities the school faces.

Establishing the Best Board Size

One of the most common questions in building a board is, "What is the right size?" The most recent NAIS governance survey identified the average size of an independent school board as 21.[5] But, in actuality, there is no right size; the right size is what works best for the needs of each particular school.

These questions can help identify the right size for the board:

- How many committees does the board have, and how many committee members are needed for each committee to complete its work on time and with appropriate quality?

- Does the board have to create special task forces to meet a short-term need of the school? Is it essential that board members serve on these task forces and, if so, what skillsets are required for this work that current board members don't already have?

- What kind of skillsets does the board need to best meet the vision and mission of the school? What gaps must be filled to create a highly effective board?

- Do current trustees feel that too much is being asked of them or that they don't have the time to manage their work?

- Does the size of the board mean that the board chair spends most of his or her time managing and communicating with the board?

The answers to these questions can begin to illuminate the right board size for a particular school. Every few years, the governance or trustee committee of the board should raise the issue of how big or small the board should be, as governance needs can change over time.

Essential Tools: Job Descriptions and Road Maps

To aid in the process of recruitment and selection, every board should develop job descriptions for trustees, committee chairs, and board officers. (For a sample board member job description and a sample trustee commitment letter, see Appendices F and G.) During the process of recruitment, board members should meet with candidate trustees to review the job description and answer any questions that those candidates might have.

It is essential that candidates understand all of the trustee roles and responsibilities before being considered for the board. Too often, trustees are elected and they then find out that the school expects them to, for example, raise a certain amount of money — a task of which they were completely unaware. Or a trustee is elected to the board, thinking that he or she is representing the voice of the parent body when it is not the role of a trustee to represent any one group.

In addition to a job description, every board should develop some sort of road map or matrix outlining the type of skills, abilities, and diversity that current members bring and in which areas the board needs to grow. These needs should guide the governance or trusteeship committee's selection of candidates for open trustee slots. Keeping this matrix current and having frequent conversations about the needs of the board is key to a highly functioning board, as new needs can frequently emerge in this quickly changing landscape. (For a sample board matrix, see Appendix H.)

Planning for Board Leadership Succession

An essential part of the talent pipeline process is planning for the succession of board leadership. Too often, boards choose their officers because of their length of service or availability for the job. Although these may be factors, boards should consider other more important criteria when selecting their leaders. The board as a whole should spend time discussing its leadership needs and ensure that it has a written board-leadership succession strategy.

An important first step in implementing that strategy is to create job descriptions for all board officers and committee chairs. (For sample qualifications for board officers, see Appendix L. For officer job descriptions, see Appendix B.) For example, the job description of the board chair should spell out not only the role of the board chair but also the desired skills and behaviors, such as "The most effective board chairs are strong in both IQ and EQ, are trustworthy, have the respect of the head and board members alike, are good listeners, and can build consensus as well as moderate healthy disagreement."

Once the board details these needs for all board officer roles, it should build a strategy for how each of those roles will be fulfilled when a key player leaves. This process begins, usually through the governance committee, by identifying leadership potential in current board members. The board chair and other board leaders should groom the members who show the greatest potential to be chairs of committees or task forces. Encouraging these trustees to serve in such positions provides an opportunity to observe how they lead.

Many boards use the role of the vice chair as the succession slot for board chair. This can be a good strategy as long as the board recruits the vice chair with that in mind. The vice chair can act as a partner with the board chair in setting strategy, planning agendas, and leading in the board chair's absence so that he or she is ready to seamlessly assume the role of chair when the time arises.

A Closing Note About Day School Trustee Recruitment

Because most day schools meet monthly throughout the school year, they tend to confine trustee selection to the local area, thus limiting their pool. NAIS recommends that they consider meeting as boarding schools do — longer meetings but less frequent — in order to open up their recruiting base to a national or even international pool of candidates. Also, with the amount of meeting technology available, boards can still get together when they need to, just virtually instead of face-to-face.

ENDNOTES

[1] Barbara E. Taylor, Richard P. Chait, and Thomas P. Holland, "The New Work of the Nonprofit Board," *Harvard Business Review*, September/October 1996; online at https://hbr.org/1996/09/the-new-work-of-the-nonprofit-board.

[2] Vernetta Walker, "Beyond Political Correctness: Building a Diverse Board," *Board Member*, May/June 2009.

[3] Mary Hundley DeKuyper, *Trustee Handbook: A Guide to Effective Governance for Independent School Boards*, 9th ed. (Washington, DC: NAIS, 2007).

[4] GreatNonprofits, "Cultivating the Ultimate Board: Interview with Kay Sprinkel Grace," Great Nonprofits Blog, January 7, 2014; online at http://greatnonprofits.org/nonprofitnews/cultivating-the-ultimate-board-interview-with-kay-sprinkel-grace/.

[5] NAIS, *Heads and Boards Working in Partnership: 2012–13 NAIS Governance Study* (Washington, DC: 2013); available in the NAIS bookstore at http://www.nais.org/bookstore.

KEY TAKEAWAYS

- Succession planning is a key role for independent school boards.
- Identifying, recruiting, and cultivating potential trustees is the work of every member of the board.
- Boards need to build a pipeline of future board talent to ensure ongoing effectiveness.
- Job descriptions for all trustee roles help ensure fit and effectiveness.
- Boards that are diverse in every way possible are the most innovative.
- Bringing outside perspective into the board is essential to seeing the school's challenges and opportunities through a holistic lens.
- Boards should choose their members as much for their leadership qualities as for their background and experience.

A Culture of Self-Assessment, Accountability, and Open Communication

EVERY SCHOOL HAS A CULTURE, and ideally that culture has been purposefully determined. Defining or strengthening a school's culture happens at every level of the school experience, among students, staff members, administrators, and board members.

The board plays an especially vital role in helping create and develop school culture by setting the tone and expectations of how the school defines and measures success. This ensures teamwork among board members and between the board and senior administrators. It also establishes collective ownership of the future of the school and enhances the amount of trust and openness that the board and administrative team exhibit with each other and the wider school community.

Once the school has set its goals and objectives, and once it is clear who is overseeing and engaged in those goals, the board must determine how it will know that progress is being made. The board should also have a sense of the overall health and operations of the school. Most boards do this through regular evaluations and assessments of themselves, the head of school, and the wider school community. This information loop helps the board and administrative team build a broader data-driven agenda, and it also provides a picture of how the school and its team as a whole are doing.

School-Wide Assessments and Evaluations

The end goal of any assessment is to answer the question: Are the school and its leadership being effective in carrying out the mission of the school? Schools use assessments and evaluations (we use the terms interchangeably) to determine whether specific progress is being made on their goals, and they may use different tools at different times to track particular advances. They have any number of assessment and evaluation instruments available to them, but they should use each one strategically to truly answer the questions that the board and school leadership have put forth.

The most widely used assessments are board evaluations and head evaluations, both of which we describe in more detail below. However, many schools have also experimented with periodic assessments of specific school-wide goals. The initial assessment provides a starting point, and then later evaluations track progress over time. This information instructs the school leaders and also gives them an opportunity to talk openly with the community about the school's successes and challenges and what it is doing to advance toward the goals.

Schools generally conduct periodic assessments through some form of survey of the elements and constituencies listed on page 57. The administration conducts these surveys, but it works with the board to determine which surveys are appropriate for the school's long-term goals and objectives. It should administer surveys on a rotating basis so that the school community does not suffer from survey fatigue.

- **Culture and climate.** These assessments can range from those that just provide student feedback to much broader tools that survey not only students but also staff members, parents, and the board.

- **Student health and well-being.** These assessments give the school a picture of the overall health and well-being of its students. They tend to be holistic and include questions about everything from anxiety, depression, and risky behaviors to homework and study loads.

- **Diversity and inclusion.** These assessments provide a window into how well the school is doing on its diversity and inclusion work, and they often give feedback that covers more general culture and climate assessment as well.

- **Alumni.** These assessments provide the school with an understanding of how well alumni feel they were prepared for life by their independent school, both academically and holistically.

- **Parents.** These assessments offer a look into parent satisfaction and can illuminate areas for improvement. While students are certainly the recipients of much of the school's efforts, parents are often each school's initial customers.

Setting Goals for Board and Head Evaluations

In order to have an effective evaluation of the board or head of school, there must be consensus and clarity on the school's overall, long-term goals. Flowing from those overall goals are annual goals and objectives, mostly informed by data and the school's mission. Ideally, schools will measure progress on these goals through completion of milestones or some other form of assessment. This allows the school leadership to see continuing advancement toward the long-term outcome.

Once the board and administration establish the school's overarching goals, they can delegate the work of accomplishing those goals as appropriate. The head of school is responsible for overseeing the implementation of certain goals and objectives among staff and will also have certain ones specifically assigned to him or her. (For sample goals for a head of school, see Appendix I.) The institution should also assign goals and objectives to the board as appropriate. Beyond these "buckets" of goals and objectives, the head of school and the board both have their standard "job descriptions" that detail their everyday duties. These elements provide the outline of responsibilities for which the head of school, the staff, and the board will all hold each other accountable. (For sample job descriptions for a trustee and a head of school, see Appendices F and J.)

Assessing the Board

Some trustees are surprised to find themselves the recipients of goals, objectives, and job descriptions in their volunteer roles. However, this level of clarity helps people understand what is expected of them and creates a better working team.

Beyond assessments and evaluations to advance the school's long-term goals and objectives, the board also needs to assess its own performance. Board assessments serve many purposes, including reminding board members of their roles and responsibilities, increasing the accountability of individual members as well as that of the board as a whole, creating a stronger team through group ownership, and confirming board members' knowledge of the school and its direction.

Most board evaluations include standard questions that align with the NAIS Principles of Good Practice (PGP) for Boards of Trustees and for Independent School Trustees. (See these PGPs on pages 9 and 10.) Board evaluation questions may cover all or some of the following areas:

- The board's work in support of the school mission

- The school's financial stability and the board's accountability and understanding of the financial position of the school

- The board's work and relationship with the head of school and administrative team

- The board's success in maintaining a long-term and strategic vision as opposed to a shorter-term more operational, tactical, or managerial focus

- The board's composition and its continuing needs in terms of skills and demographic representation

- The engagement of board members and committees

- The professional development and ongoing education of the board members

- An overview of what board members individually do or understand (preparation for meetings, financial contributions to the school, a feeling that one's skills are being used, etc.)

- Progress on particular goals or objectives, as appropriate

- Particular goals or objectives that board members think the school must address over the next few years

Many evaluation tools allow a school to add questions that reflect its particular job description for trustees so that the board members can further self-evaluate their success individually and as a group.

The evaluation should not be time-consuming, yet it can provide significant insight into the overall effectiveness of the board's structure and processes and can help solidify next steps. The evaluation can also encourage honest and open feedback from trustees who may not be as comfortable speaking out in a board meeting.

Once trustees complete the evaluation, the governance committee or executive committee reviews the results and then reports the findings and makes recommendations to the entire board. This cycle provides a feedback loop that allows the board to continue to learn and grow. Board professional development and overall work should reflect the feedback in both the board evaluation and that of the other relevant surveys.

Assessing the Head of School

One of the board's most important obligations is to hire and oversee the head of school. In terms of the long-term impact on a school's stability and the execution of its mission, oversight of the head of school may be the board's single most important undertaking. Once the board and head have agreed on the goals and objectives for the school and the head of school, an evaluation process should be straightforward and fruitful.

In most schools, the entire board participates in the head's evaluation, generally through an electronic survey. The head of school often will also fill out a self-evaluation or an overall report on the year, including progress toward meeting goals and objectives and examples of ways in which he or she has fulfilled the duties of head of school. One person on the board, often the board chair, gathers the results of the survey and the self-evaluation. Then the board chair or a small committee of the board reviews the information and presents it to the board in executive session.

If the head's compensation is tied to his or her evaluation, either as a bonus or a percentage raise for the next year, the committee may present a recommendation for that financial outcome as well. The board may debate that recommendation, ask any questions, and then vote. Depending on the school's processes, the board chair or small committee might meet with the head of school to provide him or her with the evaluation overview and receive any feedback before discussing the results with the full board. However, at some schools, this conversation will take place afterwards and often include information about any raises or bonuses as a result of the evaluation.

Some schools undertake 360-degree evaluations of the school head, whereby staff, faculty members, and others also assess him or her. If a school takes this approach, it should recognize that human resource professionals generally encourage this kind of input, particularly from staff members, as a feedback tool to build self-awareness rather than one designed to measure success and determine bonus or salary increases.

The overall structure of the head of school evaluation is similar to that of the board's evaluation, although the specific content may vary slightly. The board considers how well the head of school either oversaw the fulfillment of particular goals and objectives or accomplished his or her own particular goals, as well as how well he or she met the standard requirements of the head of school position. The NAIS Principles of Good Practice for Heads of School generally outline those standard requirements, which elements of the head of school's actual job description may augment. The evaluation may also ask for feedback in particular areas or guidance for the year ahead.

It is crucial that the head of school and the board reach an understanding before the year begins on how he or she will be evaluated and what those criteria will look like. This gives the head plenty of notice about how he or she will be assessed and avoids surprises at the end of the year. The advance notice also helps keep the board chair, as well as any small committee charged with working closely with the head of school during the school year, more aware of potential issues.

As with any good evaluation, the board should give the head of school any necessary feedback throughout the year on his or her progress and raise any potential problems before they become insurmountable. The head of school should also have the opportunity to highlight specific challenges or victories experienced during the year that may influence his or her final evaluation.

Timing and the Feedback Loop

Independent schools should use assessments not only for evaluation but also as learning opportunities. To do this, the assessments of the board and school head should be completed in time for the results to be used in creating the following year's goals and objectives — for example, at the end of the school year before details are forgotten over the summer. Goals not yet attained can be folded into the following year's goals with extra resources to help accomplish them, and goals that were reached can be surpassed with the addition of further recommended steps toward the school's overarching strategic goal.

Establishing Trust

Evaluations and assessments can make people uneasy. Therefore, creating and maintaining a culture of honesty and trust is vital to their success. From the beginning of each process to its end, all participants — including individual board members, the head of school, and every staff member — need to understand that such a process has been put in place to sustain the long-term viability and success of the school in carrying out its mission on behalf of its students. These evaluation processes must continue in a cycle of open learning, acknowledgment, accountability, and understanding to ensure that the school is using its resources in the most effective and efficient ways possible.

An assessment process also benefits from reasonable expectations, and people should be prepared to be thoughtful in setting the goals and objectives, reviewing how well they were achieved, and providing feedback on their ultimate attainment or lack thereof. Boards and heads of school can incorporate the following elements in their assessments to create and continue a culture of honesty and trust:

- **Open communication.** Both the head of school and the board need to provide regular, honest, and open communication about how both sides are progressing toward their goals, as well as where they are facing challenges. Everyone is working to attain the long-term success of the school and must communicate from a place of that shared understanding.

- **No surprises.** Any changes, transitions, challenges, mistakes, and other unpleasantness are better addressed before they become insurmountable in reality or in someone's mind. The head of school and trustees need a safe place where they can voice issues openly and without fear of retribution. In the course of the year, something will go wrong.

- **Ongoing support for the head of school.** When all is going well, it is easy to lose touch with the head of school or assume he or she does not need any help. Maintaining contact through regular meetings between the head of school and the board chair and other board members keeps the head feeling supported and heard.

- **Non-meeting events.** Building a culture of trust and openness takes effort, including some time away from the board table. Creating opportunities for camaraderie and taking the time to gather apart from official meetings reminds everyone that we are people first and heads and trustees second.

- **Disclosure to community.** School leadership teams have learned time and time again that hiding issues from the school community rarely, if ever, works out well. Students, parents, staff members, and alumni all generally want to see the institution succeed. They are more likely to support it during challenging times if they feel that its leaders are open and honest in their communications about those challenges.

Board Development

Board growth is aided by a culture of continual assessment, yet it is nurtured by a commitment to ongoing board professional development. A board that learns together has a shared understanding of best governance practices, the challenges and opportunities facing the school, and the larger world in which the school operates. Building this kind of consistent knowledge among all board members makes for more informed decision making and can set the stage for operating effectively in all three modes of governance. The governance committee (or committee on trustees) usually oversees this process, beginning with an orientation for new trustees.

New Trustee Orientation

An annual new trustee orientation is the foundation of good governance practice, ensuring that board members understand what it means to serve on a nonprofit board, their roles and responsibilities as trustees, and the strategic priorities of the school. In addition, it is an opportunity to acquaint trustees with the culture and operating procedures of the board, including the school's bylaws and policies. A comprehensive orientation can also include an introduction to the main issues facing the independent school sector overall. Sometimes schools ignore the orientation process, assuming that new board members are well acquainted with the school. This is a mistake, as it can signal that taking time to learn is not valued by the board, as well as leave new trustees with significant information gaps.

Ongoing Training

In addition to orientation, healthy boards carve out time in the schedule for professional development throughout the year by any or all of the following means:

- Attending professional development events offered by school or governance organizations. (NAIS offers a governance track at its annual conference and an institute for board chairs and heads in the fall.)

- Listening to presentations by outside experts on topics such as the changing recruitment market or new financial models for schools.

- Reading governance and trend publications together as a board and taking time to discuss the implications for the school. (Reading Chait, Ryan, and Taylor's *Governance as Leadership* together as a board can be a good basis for understanding what it means to operate effectively in the three different modes of governance. NAIS's annual *Trendbook* can acquaint trustees with changing trends that can impact the school in the coming year.)

- Hiring a facilitator to lead the board through the results of the annual assessment, spurring discussion about areas for growth and development.

- Participating in webinars or listening to podcasts on topics of interest.

Professional development can also be tied to annual board goals. For example, if the board adopts a goal to develop a five-year financial plan, professional development throughout the year can focus on issues such as these:

- A comprehensive review, analysis, and discussion of the school's financial trends over the last decade

- A presentation on changing demographic and economic trends in the region that can affect the school's financial health

- Research on and discussion of new school financial models

- A presentation on the competitive landscape for independent schools in the region

Whatever form it takes, professional development is an essential building block in the foundation of an effective board.

A Final Word on Building the Best Culture

The extent to which the school community as a whole creates an open, honest, accountable, and trusting culture depends on every level of the school embracing it. Schools assess and evaluate students every day and encourage them to learn from those outcomes as part of their educational cycle. For students to truly understand the importance of that cycle, they need to see adults in positions of power embody it. Board members and heads of schools have the ability to model the behavior they want to see in students through their own governance and management processes.

KEY TAKEAWAYS

- Schools use any number of assessments to track their progress toward fulfilling their missions and achieving long-term goals and objectives.

- Goal-setting should focus on both long-term and short-term goals and objectives and involve the head of school and the board.

- The board should conduct annual self-evaluations and include the key points of the relevant NAIS Principles of Good Practice as well as any board-specific goals and objectives for that year.

- A school should assess its head of school annually and include the key points of the relevant Principles of Good Practice along with any specific goals and objectives for the year.

- A school should establish evaluation processes and metrics before the beginning of the fiscal year so that the head of school and board have a concrete understanding of what's expected of them.

- A successful goal-setting and evaluation process is grounded in trust, openness, and regular communications. All players are on the same team and must operate from that place.

- The board and head of school must work together to ensure that a culture of trust, honesty, and openness exists at the leadership level, and they should model that behavior for the rest of the school and the wider community.

- The board should take the time to learn together, making trustee orientation and ongoing professional development at the core of their work.

- This openness should be transparent to the wider community in how the board communicates about its practices, the story of the school, and the challenges the school may face.

A Structure That Supports Efficiency and Innovation

HOW A BOARD IS STRUCTURED and operates can predict how effective it will be. Most boards function well at the fiduciary level, developing policy and ensuring legal compliance and financial health. But they often falter in the strategic and generative modes because they don't have a structure or a way of operating that nurtures these modes. To change that trajectory, school boards should dissect their structures and operating processes and discuss what helps and hinders them. This includes committee and task force structures, board meeting operations, and when and how often the board meets.

In addition to the information in this chapter, the NAIS book *Doing More with Less: How Committees and Task Forces Can Strengthen Your Board* offers detailed guidance on the role of committees and task forces.

The Role of Board Committees

Board committees play an important role in the life of the board. The board accomplishes much of its planning and tactical work through its committees, allowing time when all members come together for more strategic work. Independent school boards have traditionally operated with the following standing committees:

- **The executive committee** is generally made up of board officers and committee chairs and can function in place of the full board if the board cannot meet on a particular issue. This committee also takes the lead in planning the board's agenda and usually oversees the head's evaluation and compensation processes. Boards need to be careful that executive committees don't overstep and undermine the healthy functioning of the full board.

- **The finance committee** ensures the long-term financial health of the school and reviews and approves the annual budget. This committee also creates financial policies, such as the investment policy. The finance committee may also investigate the creation of alternative revenue streams. Generally, a separate audit committee may report to the finance committee.

- **The governance committee** (sometimes called the committee on trustees or nominating committee) oversees the growth and development of the board. This committee is responsible for succession planning; trustee identification, recruitment, cultivation, and selection; board assessment; and board education. This group is usually responsible for new trustee orientation.

- **The development committee** sets the annual goals for fundraising and monitors all fund-raising activities of the school to ensure that they meet those goals. This committee also takes the lead in educating trustees about their role in fund-raising and fund-raising techniques and involves them in the fund-raising process.

- **The buildings and grounds committee** oversees the growth and development of the school's plant and grounds, including stewarding the master plan and determining how assets are allocated to both maintain and enhance the school's physical plant.

Other types of standing committees found on independent school boards include diversity, strategic planning, marketing, education, enrollment management, and ethics.

Although independent school boards have employed such a committee structure for decades, in *Governance as Leadership*, Chait, Ryan, and Taylor point out that nonprofits tend to create board committees that mirror organizational structures, and this often pulls trustees into a tactical rather than a strategic approach. The authors advise, "Constructed and organized in this way, boards are predisposed, if not predestined, to attend to the routine, technical work."[1]

Many schools today are moving toward altering the committee structure in a way that promotes a more strategic approach. For example, at one school, the board retired both the finance committee and the buildings and grounds committee and created instead a new committee called the assets committee. The idea was to engage the board in a much higher-level discussion on how assets were acquired and used in service of the school's vision. A board member described the change:

> The dynamics of very small, focused committees can become stagnant and ineffective, often leading to topic-fatigue and tunnel-vision. By increasing membership and making the discourse more interdisciplinary, trustees have become more engaged and more aware of the context and interconnectedness of our work.

> The newfound breadth of the conversation reveals informa-
> tion and insight into the school more broadly, thus empowering
> trustees and instilling a level of trust that comes with seeing the
> "big-picture" together.[2]

AGB has developed the "AGB Effective Committee Series," which
provides general advice to focus the work of various board committees. It recommends that each committee have a clear charter outlining its purpose; that committee work align with the institution's
strategic vision, goals, and priorities; and that committees translate
their charges into annual work plans that reinforce the institution's
strategic objectives. It goes on to note that committee members
should strike an appropriate balance between asking for too much
information — and overburdening and micromanaging staff — or
too little information — whereby they lack "sufficient supporting
materials to make sound recommendations and ensure adequate
oversight." Finally, it advises that committee agendas be concise,
state desired outcomes clearly, and be distributed well in advance.[3]
(See a sample board meeting agenda in Appendix L.)

The Role of Task Forces

Unlike committees, which are standing from year to year, any task
force that the board establishes should have a specific mission and a
clear start and end date. Although task forces usually include some
trustees as members, they also offer the opportunity to bring in non-
board experts. In recent years, schools have moved toward creating
fewer standing committees and more task forces. Generally, these
task forces focus on the school's pressing challenges, new opportunities, or future planning.

According to NAIS's latest governance research, more than 90 percent of independent school boards create task forces on a routine basis. The most popular task forces by far relate to strategic planning and visioning for their schools. Following strategic planning in terms of popularity are task forces related to marketing or communications. A number of schools also have task forces relating to the head search or succession planning.[4]

In a *Harvard Business Review* article about the new work of nonprofit boards, Taylor, Chait, and Holland provide a case study of a college board that retreats every January to discuss, with the president, the major challenges and opportunities facing the institution. The board then creates task forces to deal with the new business or concentrates committee agendas primarily on these issues. These "tissue paper" (use and discard) task forces drive the board toward real-time results, multiply leadership opportunities, and prevent longtime members from dominating standing committees.[5]

The Consent Agenda Model

Boards have limited time to do their work, so they should focus their time together on those issues that hold the most value to the school's growth and development. Generally, the board can accomplish most of its tactical work in committees. It should reserve the time that all board members spend together for strategic or generative conversations or for board education and development.

The easiest way to accomplish this is to adopt a consent agenda model for board meetings. In this model, the board bundles together committee reports, minutes, and other routine business into one item for approval. To do this, boards must adopt the following three practices:

1. Committees must distribute meeting minutes well ahead of board meetings so that trustees have the time to read and absorb the materials.

2. Trustees must take the time to read the materials in advance.

3. All board members must understand the rules that govern a consent agenda so that it is clear which items may be placed on the consent agenda, as well as the process for taking an item from the agenda and putting it back on the regular agenda for discussion.

Another reason why consent agendas can be effective in driving a strategic orientation is that they focus the board's attention on the future rather than on events or decisions that have already occurred. Items from committee reports are often merely a summation of previous activities with little opportunity for board discussion or for any action that might have an impact. Once a board moves to the consent agenda approach, it opens up its time for the strategic work that should be central to its operations.

Indicators of Success

Every year, the board should work together with the head of school to set goals for the head and for itself. The goals of the board and the head should reinforce each other and support the mission and vision of the school. When setting goals, boards also should establish some sort of performance measures. For the head, this will help define what success looks like in the board's view, and for the board, it will create discipline that will keep it focused on outcomes.

In conjunction with these measures, the board, working with the head of school, should establish a set of indicators that will assist it in monitoring the health of the institution. These indicators could cover trends in areas such as the following:

- Enrollment
- Student attrition
- The budget
- Faculty attrition
- Diversity
- Fund-raising

NAIS, through its Data and Analysis for School Leadership (DASL) platform, has established a series of dashboards that schools can use to monitor their own trends over time or in relation to a set of benchmark schools. Schools can access all of the customizable dashboards through the NAIS website at http://dasl.nais.org.

Another approach to monitoring the health of the school is to pull together indicators that measure particular ways in which the institution is meeting its goals. For example, the board and school leadership can create an efficiency score by looking at indicators like expense per student or the student-teacher ratio and assigning low, average, and high efficiency ratings to different ranges of scores. If the goal is to move the needle in a particular area, such as school efficiency, this can be an effective way to monitor growth or decline. Whatever the approach, boards that measure their performance, and that of the head of school, will become much more focused on what needs to be done to secure the long-term health and welfare of the school.

Scheduling Meetings and Retreats

Although seemingly a mundane issue, *when* a board schedules its meetings can contribute to its effectiveness. As a rule, boarding schools hold meetings for longer periods of time (for example, over a weekend), but they meet far less often than day schools. Day school boards tend to meet once a month for nine months, generally in the late afternoon or early evening. When asked why they meet so often, day school boards will respond that they have too much work to meet less frequently.

But are the issues of day schools more complex than those that boarding schools face? Probably not. The reason for these numerous meetings, in many cases, is that too much time is spent on things that don't matter or that occurred in the past. And meeting late in the afternoon, often after board members have spent a long day at work, means that the board is not coming together at a time of high energy.

Boards that take time to meet in a retreat fashion often find that the time and setting spur the kind of high energy and imaginative thinking that drive innovation. Chait, Taylor, and Holland advise that the work of nonprofit boards today should have four major characteristics:

1. It should concern itself with crucial, do-or-die issues central to the institution's success.

2. It must be driven by results that are linked to defined timetables.

3. It must have clear measures of success.

4. It should require the engagement of the school's internal and external constituencies. The work generates high levels of interest and demands broad participation and widespread support.[6]

Governance and Innovation

As the work of governance becomes more complex in this quickly changing education landscape, boards will be called on more often to innovate. Are there ways that boards should structure themselves to nurture innovation?

In recent years, researchers have studied this topic. In a 2012 article in *Nonprofit Management and Leadership,* Kristina Jaskyte explored governance research from the past decade to uncover the drivers for boards that spur organizational innovation. She identified two separate paths that could influence innovation: one focusing on the board's processes and the other on the board's makeup and structure. Within these two frameworks, Jaskyte identified several areas that boards should consider to drive organizational innovation. Among the ideas most relevant in the independent school setting:

- Boards should set goals and priorities for innovation, provide freedom to come up with new ideas, and approve innovative proposals.

- Boards can challenge a school head to support innovation and monitor his or her efforts. Board members should consider how to spur a head to become more innovative when constructing annual goals.

- When pursuing innovation, a school should align the interests of its head with those of the board, because both parties have a say over resource allocation. Overall board effectiveness results when the board and head share a common vision of how to achieve the school's goals. (For a Sample Goals Action Plan, see Appendix M.)

- The effects of board size on school innovation can be both positive and negative. A large board means a greater pool of potential school supporters, as well as higher visibility in the local community. But as a board's size increases, it can experience group-dynamic problems associated with large groups. Schools need to monitor this closely to establish the optimum board size for their work.

- Boards with high expectations and standards will tend to perform their tasks more effectively. Thus, boards should set high standards and stretch goals for all board members.[7]

ENDNOTES

[1] Richard P. Chait, William P. Ryan, Barbara E. Taylor, *Governance as Leadership: Reframing the Work of Nonprofit Boards* (Washington, DC: BoardSource, 2005).

[2] Personal communication to the authors.

[3] Association of Governing Boards of Universities and Colleges, "Effective Committee Series."

[4] NAIS, *Heads and Boards Working in Partnership: 2012–13 NAIS Governance Study* (Washington, DC: 2013); available in the NAIS bookstore at http://www.nais.org/bookstore.

[5] Barbara E. Taylor, Richard P. Chait, and Thomas P. Holland, "The New Work of the Nonprofit Board," *Harvard Business Review*, September/ October 1996; online at https://hbr.org/1996/09/the-new-work-of-the-nonprofit-board.

[6] Ibid.

[7] Kristina Jaskyte, "Boards of Directors and Innovation in Nonprofit Organizations," *Nonprofit Management and Leadership*, Summer 2012; online at http://onlinelibrary.wiley.com/doi/10.1002/nml.21039/pdf.

KEY TAKEAWAYS

- A board's structure and style of operations directly impact its ability to be strategic and generative.

- There is a growing trend to limit the number of board committees and instead create task forces around pressing issues or opportunities.

- Consent agenda models can free up needed time at board meetings for strategic discussions or board education.

- Setting goals and performance measures is essential to effective governance.

- Scheduling board meetings in retreat-like settings can move board discussions from the tactical to the strategic.

- The makeup of the board and how it operates can have a direct impact on its ability to innovate.

7

▪ The Independent School Context

CHANGE IS EVER-PRESENT in the education landscape of today. To govern effectively through change, trustees need to know more than the Principles of Good Practice for Boards. They must also have a deep understanding of the context in which independent schools operate. Three issues are of vital importance: (1) the market from which schools recruit, (2) the financial model that underpins a school's fiscal health, and (3) the larger education landscape in which they exist.

The Market

The school market of today is quite different than it was in the 1990s. At that time, there was double-digit growth in the school-age population,[1] and the educational choices were primarily the assigned public school or a private school. Today, the growth of the school-age population has slowed, even declining in some parts of the country, and the makeup of that population is changing. While once that population was majority white, it is increasingly moving toward a majority minority, with the fastest growth in the Asian and Hispanic populations.

The market is also far more competitive now, with new types of schools appearing on the horizon every day. There are now public charter schools, public magnet schools, for-profit private schools, schools run by major corporations, online schools, and home-schooling. Some people are even pursuing DIY (do-it-yourself) education in which they choose from all the options to create an approach custom-tailored to each of their children's needs. This could mean homeschooling supplemented by specialized tutors, with some coursework done online through a provider like Kahn Academy or a virtual charter school.

These changing market forces create a more complex enrollment scenario for independent schools. Trustees need to have a comprehensive understanding of their school's current and potential markets in order to make informed strategic decisions for it. What information should they be reviewing? How can they get up to speed quickly on the key issues?

Below are the major data points or trends that will assist trustees in this process:

- **Demographic changes.** School boards should examine yearly data on demographic shifts in their recruiting area, as well as any predicted changes. They should monitor data points on the number of school-age children by race and ethnicity, gender, and family income and look for forecasted growth or decline.

  Day schools should analyze the data by zip code, particularly if they are reliant on two or three surrounding zip codes for the majority of their students. NAIS member schools can track all these data points free of charge on the web-based NAIS Demographic Center (available at http://www.nais.org).

  Another area of demographic change is the economic health of families in the region. Data points on employment and housing values can be helpful indicators of change. If the area has one or more dominant employers or industries, it is important to monitor how they are faring financially. NAIS's Demographic Center and Demographic Snapshot (available at http://www.nais.org) list basic economic indicators. Boards can find more comprehensive regional economic data through a variety of services, such as Moody's State Analytic Services (http://www.economy.com/regions/us-states-and-metro-areas).

- **Admissions trends.** Every trustee should be familiar with the school's admissions trends and how those trends have changed over time. At least once every year, boards should engage in generative conversations about such data and explore what opportunities or challenges they present. Of particular value is viewing a school's admissions trends in conjunction with all other independent schools in the recruiting area and, in particular, with top competing schools. Trustees should look for similarities and differences in those trends to identify the challenges or opportunities that are particular to their school.

- **Competition.** Board members should be aware of other schools in the recruitment area, know the array of school types available (including those that are virtual), and understand which institutions are top competitors. In this quickly changing landscape, boards should be tracking new entrants into their markets. For example, many major metropolitan areas have seen a growth in new, low-cost, for-profit private schools.

- **Constituent satisfaction data.** Every school should be conducting periodic parent satisfaction surveys and sharing that information with its trustees. These surveys can identify what families most value in their children's educational experience and how well they perceive the school is delivering it. Having this kind of data helps trustees understand what resource investments they need to make to ensure market satisfaction.

With that said, every school should have a mission and vision statement that guides its growth and development. While the school should be seen as having a distinct value in the marketplace, it must also be careful not to become so market driven that it tries to be all things to all people or loses sight of its own identity.

- **Image assessment data.** Hand in glove with the parent satisfaction data are analyses of how people view the school compared with other educational options in the market. These studies, also known as "brand value studies," can be expensive, but they can also be especially useful in uncovering what the market sees as a particular school's value. NAIS has a research partner, Rockbridge Associates, that offers a brand value study for independent schools (http://www.rockresearch.com/nais-school-study/).

- **Consumer trends.** Finally, it is useful for boards to be aware of consumer trends that can drive what the market values at a particular time. Usually, boards can uncover these trends through routine environmental scanning or by reading trend publications, such as the *NAIS Trendbook*. Published annually, the *Trendbook* can be ordered through NAIS's website (http://www.nais.org/bookstore).

The Financial Model

A key responsibility of every trustee is to ensure the short- and long-term financial health and well-being of the school. That begins with understanding the financial model that underpins the school. Most independent schools have four major sources of operating funds: (1) tuition and fees, (2) charitable donations, (3) auxiliary programs, and (4) income from investments (which may include endowment income). Some schools also run outside businesses or engage in partnerships that bring in non-tuition revenue.

In a changing demographic and economic landscape, building and managing the school budget has become a much more complex endeavor than in the past. Therefore, it has never been more important that trustees understand the drivers of financial health and the perils of the current financial model — which may depend too heavily on factors that economic difficulties can negatively influence.

For example, after the 2008 recession, many schools faced the double blow of a downturn in both enrollment and charitable gifts. Without other revenue sources to stay afloat, many had to make tough budget decisions. They responded by trimming operational costs, deferring physical plant improvements, freezing salaries, increasing financial aid, and raising tuition. For many schools, such decisions have had long-term negative impacts. For example, some schools have now priced themselves out of significant segments of their markets.

In a 2013 study that NAIS conducted to identify the factors that determine the educational choices of higher-income parents (those with an annual income of at least $75K), the cost of tuition was the top driver in the choice between independent schools and other options. The following areas also influenced decisions:

- Teacher quality
- A focus on building students of character, morals, and values
- Preparation for future success
- School reputation

The study also found that although a high tuition may dissuade parents from choosing independent schools, this barrier can be somewhat overcome. How? By convincing parents that the independent school is well-established, has high-quality and dedicated teachers, focuses on building students of character, and provides excellent preparation for the future success of students.[2]

The soaring costs of tuition have also limited socioeconomic diversity at independent schools. With fewer families able to afford the high cost of tuition in some areas of the country, independent schools are spending financial aid budgets primarily to meet enrollment goals rather than to provide socioeconomic diversity. Schools have always prized diversity, and research has documented its value in providing positive student outcomes. But the tuition costs of many schools have limited their ability to build diverse school communities.

Finally, freezing salaries has impacted the school workforce. With increasing shortages in some areas of the skilled workforce and the changing motivations of those entering the education field, schools may find it harder to compete for high-quality teachers and administrators. For example, much of the research around new teachers entering the workforce indicates that they are looking for a pay-for-performance model of compensation.

Board members need to understand all of the forces that are

influencing the current financial model and devote time to discussing how they can change that model to ensure a more sustainable future.

Schools today are exploring new ways to create a more stable model, such as the following:

- Developing partnerships that can fund new programming
- Creating auxiliary businesses that drive additional sources of revenue
- Using technology to cut operational costs — for example, offering online courses as part of a consortium instead of hiring additional faculty
- Buying services as part of a consortium to save costs
- Increasing the student-teacher ratio
- Eliminating costly facilities, such as swimming pools, and taking advantage of community facilities instead

With lower-cost educational options entering the market every day and continued volatility in the economy, boards will need to devote more time and resources to creating and managing a more sustainable financial model for independent schools.

The Education Landscape

Another area about which board members should be knowledgeable is the larger education landscape in which K–12 independent schools operate. The entire context in which education exists has changed, with the proliferation of new and different types of schools in the education marketplace, the explosive growth of technology, and massive changes in higher education.

Technology is ushering in a new way of educating students. From fully online schools to hybrid programs (a mix of online and face-to-face) to flipped classrooms, schools of all sizes and grade levels are experimenting with technology to enhance access and learning. In the independent school world, online and hybrid learning programs are being employed to accomplish certain aims:

- Supplement existing curricula
- Maximize the respective strengths of online and face-to-face learning
- Prepare students for online college and university courses
- Keep students engaged in learning
- Address students' scheduling conflicts
- Meet a student's special interest
- Keep a school running during a natural disaster or unusual circumstances
- Engage in global outreach
- Meet the needs of students with learning differences
- Enhance revenue[3]

Schools are offering these programs either individually or as part of consortia such as the Online School for Girls or the Global Online Academy.

Technology has also driven enormous change in higher education. We saw the advent of many online colleges in the 1990s, the rise of the MOOCs (massive open online courses) in 2008, and growing interest in competency-based education in the last few years. According to the U.S. Department of Education, competency-based education means

> transitioning away from seat time, in favor of a structure that creates flexibility, [which] allows students to progress as they demonstrate mastery of academic content, regardless of time, place, or pace of learning. Competency-based strategies provide flexibility in the way that credit can be earned or awarded, and provide students with personalized learning opportunities.[4]

A growing number of colleges and universities are testing out this approach, either as a fully online program or a blended approach with some face-to-face class time.

There are critics on both sides of the fence. Some feel that these experiments will not take root, while others believe we are on the cusp of a revolution. In his book *The End of College: Creating the Future of Learning and the University of Everywhere*, Kevin Carey explains how two trends — the skyrocketing cost of college and the revolution in information technology — are converging in ways that will radically alter the college experience.[5] On the K–12 front, the ground-breaking book *Disrupting Class: How Disruptive Innovation Will Change the Way the World Learns* engaged the principles of disruptive innovation to explore a student-centric learning model fueled by technology.[6]

Another element of change is the growing view among employers that college graduates are not prepared for the workforce. In numerous studies, employers lament that college graduates are ill-equipped to write clearly, manage a project, give a presentation, conduct a meeting, or create a budget.

What does this mean for boards of independent schools? First and foremost, it signals an opportunity for governance to play a crucial role in transforming education in the service of every child. Never before have we known so much about how the brain works or had access to tools to customize education to the needs of individual learners. With the *independence* of independent schools, boards now have an opportunity to create and invest in a system of education that knows no bounds.

Additionally, with the changes occurring in higher education, boards have an unprecedented chance to rethink the part that K–12 education plays in the growth and development of a child. What is the role of a college prep school in a society in which college may no longer be the aspiration?

And, finally, what is the financial model that will ensure the health and well-being of our schools while providing access to a growing number of students? Effective board structures fueled by an innovative, diverse group of trustees can lead the way.

Conclusion

The landscape in which schools exist today calls for a different kind of governance. Boards must take care of their fiduciary obligations, but it does not end there. To best serve independent schools today, boards must:

- be strategic in their orientation;

- use data to guide their work and assess their performance;

- be as diverse as possible and encourage diversity of opinion;

- spend time only on those things that matter most to the health and well-being of the school;

- structure themselves for innovation;

- know the world that they serve and bring in experts to inform that knowledge; and

- develop themselves continually in service to the school.

ENDNOTES

[1] U.S. Census Bureau, "Age 2000," October 2001; online at http://www.census.gov/prod/2001pubs/c2kbr01-12.pdf.

[2] Amada Torres, "Charter School Parents and Their Perceptions of Independent Schools," *Independent School* Magazine, Fall 2014; online at http://www.nais.org/TrusteeHandbook.

[3] NAIS, *Hybrid/Blended Learning in Independent Schools* (Washington, DC: 2011); online at http://www.nais.org/TrusteeHandbook.

[4] U.S. Department of Education, "Competency-Based Learning or Personalized Learning"; online at http://www.ed.gov/oii-news/competency-based-learning-or-personalized-learning.

[5] Kevin Carey, *The End of College: Creating the Future of Learning and the University of Everywhere* (New York: Riverhead Books, 2015)

[6] Clayton M. Christensen, Michael B. Horn, and Curtis W. Johnson, *Disrupting Class: How Disruptive Innovation Will Change the Way the World Learns* (New York: McGraw Hill, 2008)

KEY TAKEAWAYS

- To govern effectively, trustees must be knowledgeable about the context in which independent schools currently exist.

- Three areas are particularly important: the school's recruiting market, its financial model, and the larger landscape of education today.

- To best understand the school market, trustees must have access to demographic data, attitudinal studies, and consumer trend research.

- To best understand the financial model, trustees should be well versed about the school's financial structure and the strengths and weaknesses of that structure.

- Technology is opening many doors, and board members need to understand both the opportunities and the challenges it brings.

- The changes in higher education will require independent school boards to think in exciting new ways about the role of K–12 education.

Appendices

APPENDIX A

Sample Calendar of Board Meetings

AUGUST

Head of school and administrative team meet to identify this year's primary goals, particularly those goals and objectives where board support is crucial.

Head of school and board chair meet to review overall goals and objectives for school, as well as agree on current and potential goals and objectives for board. Board chair and head of school develop the following calendar based on the school's identified goals of greater enrollment, greater diversity, and the development of alternative revenue streams. The individual committees will also develop calendars reflecting these aims, particularly the advancement, finance, and strategy and initiatives committees.

SEPTEMBER

New Trustee Orientation

Opening Board Meeting

Strategic Focus:
• The Admissions Marketplace (report from Enrollment and Financial Sustainability Task Forces)

Board Business:
• Head of School Goals, Overall School Goals
• Results of Board Assessment
• Discussion of Board Education Needs

OCTOBER

Education Sessions:
• Building a diverse and welcoming school community
• Learning differences in our school

Board Business:
• Preliminary Budget Presentation
• Adoption of Policies

NOVEMBER

Strategic Focus:
• Report from Financial Sustainability Task Force
  and conversation

Board Business:
• Building the Budget
• Report from Development

DECEMBER

Optional budget meeting if needed

JANUARY

Strategic Focus:
• Mid-year check on goals and objectives for board and
  planning for remainder of academic year.

Board Business:
• Audit Report
• Mid-Year Update on Head of School Goals
• Adoption of the Budget

FEBRUARY

Education Session:
• The needs of the 21st century marketplace and how our
  school compares

Strategic Focus:
• Marketing the school in a changing marketplace
  (reports from Enrollment and Financial Sustainability Task Forces)

MARCH

Education Session:
• Enrollment management during challenging times

Strategic Focus:
• Enrollment challenges and opportunities

Board Business:
• Development Update

APRIL

Education Session:
• Our school's salaries and benefits in this marketplace

Strategic Focus:
• The coming challenges of teacher recruitment and retention

Board Business:
• Selection of New Trustees

MAY

Strategic Focus:
• Final Recommendations from Enrollment and
  Financial Sustainability Task Forces

Board Business:
• Celebration of Retiring Trustees
• Assessment Instructions and Timetable
• Calendar/Focus for Next Year

APPENDIX B

Duties of Board Leaders (Sample Language)

BOARD CHAIR

The chair is the senior volunteer leader of the school who sets the tone and direction for the board and presides at all meetings of the board, the executive committee, and other meetings as required. The chair generally is an ex officio member of all committees of the board. The board chair leads and manages the board, keeps the board focused on the most strategic issues, implements board policies, and ensures that appropriate board processes are established and maintained.

Key Responsibilities:

- Partners with the head of school to ensure that the board is addressing the most imperative strategic issues.

- Leads the board in establishing annual goals for its work.

- Works with the school head, board officers, and committee chairs to develop the agendas for board meetings, and presides at those meetings.

- Supports annual fund-raising with his or her own financial contributions.

- Works with the board, in accordance with the school's bylaws, to establish and maintain systems for the following:

  - Evaluating and compensating the head of school.
  - Ensuring the long-term financial health of the school.
  - Ensuring that school programs and services remain in line with the mission.
  - Acquiring, maintaining, and disposing of school property.
  - Maintaining proper risk management.
  - Ensuring that ethical and legal standards are met.

- Overseeing the growth and development of the board.

- Ensuring adequate board succession planning.

VICE CHAIR

The vice chair is a key partner with the board chair and the head of school in setting the strategic direction for the board. He or she presides over board activities in the chair's absence, is a key liaison to committees, and leads special board initiatives as agreed upon with the chair. Generally, the vice chair will assume the chairmanship of the board following the end of the current chair's term; thus, the vice chair should be chosen with a view to the chair's responsibilities as well.

Key Responsibilities:

- Works with the board chair and head of school to develop the annual strategic agenda for the school.

- Presides at meetings of the board and the executive committee in the absence of the chair.

- Serves as a member of the governance committee and other standing committees as needed.

- Assists the chair in leading the process for evaluating and compensating the head of school.

- When the school is in active strategic planning mode, chairs the committee or task force of the board.

BOARD SECRETARY

The board secretary ensures that a legal record is kept of all board proceedings and that all required notices, as specified by the school's bylaws or by state or federal law, are given in accordance.

Key Responsibilities:

- Provides the complete agenda to all board members in advance of the board meeting, as well as appropriate background information on subjects to be discussed.

- Prepares and provides written minutes to board members and ensures that a record of all minutes are kept by the school.

- Ensures that all changes to the bylaws are updated and recorded as required.

- Ensures that all notices are given in accordance with the provisions of the school's bylaws or as required by law.

BOARD TREASURER

The treasurer, jointly with the board chair, works in partnership with the head of school to ensure the short- and long-term fiscal health and welfare of the school. He or she also ensures that proper financial records are kept, that appropriate investment strategies are implemented, and that the annual operating budget of the school is developed and approved to support the strategic priorities of the school.

Key Responsibilities:

- Works with the finance committee in the preparation of the annual operating budget.

- Serves as the chair of the finance committee (usually).

- Ensures that accurate books and records on the school's financial condition are maintained.

- Ensures that the school's assets are protected and invested according to policy.

- Ensures that the school complies with statutory reporting requirements.

- Ensures that comprehensive financial reports to the board are prepared in a timely and accurate manner.

- Ensures that the complete records of the school are available to the individual or individuals preparing the annual financial statements.

COMMITTEE CHAIRS

General Responsibilities

- Set the agenda for and preside over committee meetings.
- Work in partnership with the board chair and head of school to ensure that committee agendas are in sync with the strategic goals of the board.
- Record decisions and recommendations made by the committee.
- Serve on the executive committee.
- Report the committee's activities and recommendations to the executive committee and the full board.
- Oversee succession planning for the committee, in conjunction with the board chair and the head of school.
- Delegate responsibilities to other committee members and encourage their full participation.
- Evaluate the work of the committee with other committee officers, the board chair, and the head.

APPENDIX C
Board Manual Contents

BOARD MEMBERSHIP AND CALENDAR

- List of trustees with names, preferred addresses for mail and email, preferred phone and fax numbers, short biographies
- Board and committee job descriptions
- List of officers, with titles
- Committee lists, including names and addresses of non-trustee members
- Calendar of board and committee meetings and any other meetings or functions at which trustee attendance is expected (for the fiscal or administrative year)

ORGANIZATIONAL BACKGROUND INFORMATION

- Mission, vision, and values and/or philosophy statements
- Short history of the school, including how it was established, major events, and individuals involved at critical decision points
- Description of the total program
- Description of the student body
- Strategic plan
- Most recent annual report
- Public relations material, especially those items describing the school's program and facilities
- Organizational chart

BYLAWS AND POLICIES

- Articles of incorporation, corporate charter, and bylaws
- Board policies on conflicts of interest, attendance at meetings, indemnification/directors and officers liability, reimbursement for expenses, giving and getting, etc.

ADMINISTRATION/FACULTY

- List of administrators (with titles), faculty, and staff
- Faculty handbook (or where board members can access it)
- Job descriptions of key administrators (or where they can be accessed)
- Personnel policies, including evaluation process (or where they can be accessed)

STUDENTS

- Student handbook
- School student/parent list
- Two or three issues of the student newspaper

FINANCES

- Financial policies and procedures, including investment policy (or where they can be accessed)
- Budget
- Long-range financial plan
- Most recent independent audit report
- Annual fund-raising plan
- Periodic financial reports (if separate from minutes)

MINUTES AND ISSUE DESCRIPTIONS

- Minutes of several board meetings
- Brief description of issues facing the school, especially those that involve the board

RESOURCES

- Bibliography on trusteeship
- Local, state, or regional independent school associations
- National Association of Independent Schools
- NAIS's *Trustee Handbook*
- NAIS's Principles of Good Practice (for independent school trustees, for boards of trustees, and for equity and justice)

APPENDIX D
Major Board and Administrative Policy Checklists

Different schools adopt different written policies. Even so, the following lists serve as a useful point of departure for considering the types of policies your board and staff need.

Three efficiency hints:

(1) When compiling board meeting minutes, always print statements of board policy in **bold** or CAPITAL LETTERS to make them easily traceable.

(2) Simplify the way you track board decisions by creating a cover sheet for each set of minutes with all actions noted and described. This cover sheet can also be kept in a separate file in the school office so that you only need to search one location to find out what was decided when.

(3) Make sure that new trustee orientations include either copies of the relevant minutes or a separate policy statement document list, with dates when policies were passed, reaffirmed, etc.

Broad institutional policies for which responsibility rests with the board of trustees

- A clear school mission statement, philosophy of education and/or statement of values, and vision statement

- Up-to-date bylaws

- Conflict-of-interest statements (forms that trustees and administrators sign annually to acknowledge the policies and identify real and potential conflicts)

- Strategic plan with measurable action items (as opposed to operational plans, which are usually the responsibility of the administration and faculty)

- Rolling three-year financial plan
- Crisis management plan
- Authorization or delegation of authority by the board to the head

Policies for which responsibility rests with the board of trustees and the head

- Safety and security of the school community
- Data security
- Adequate insurance coverage (including general liability and coverage for directors and officers)
- Personnel (including compensation, salary ranges, faculty course load, protection from sexual harassment, whistle-blower protection)
- Admissions (preferences, if any; desired school population to serve; size of student body)
- Financial aid (categories of eligibility; merit or need-based or both)
- Financial management, especially checks and balances
- Investment management, spending rate, etc.
- Bonds for paid staff and volunteers who handle money
- Document retention
- Bids required for contract goods and services

APPENDIX E

Risk Management Checklist

Every board should evaluate risk regularly. The following checklist provides a starting point to help you prepare.

- Clear mission statement
- Crisis management plan
- A system to review policies periodically, both internally and with outside professional assistance
- Up-to-date bylaws
- A strategic plan that has measurable action plans
- A rolling three-year financial plan

Adequate insurance:

- General liability
- Directors and officers liability

Written policies in these areas:

- Blood-borne pathogens
- Conflicts of interest, with forms signed by trustees and administrators acknowledging the policy and identifying potential conflicts
- Personnel: hiring, evaluation, termination
- Staff evaluation and compensation (especially in regard to IRS intermediate sanctions provisions)
- Student code of conduct and discipline procedures
- Religious activity on campus
- Athletic safety

- Use of school bulletin boards
- Off-campus trips — including policies about adult supervision — locally, nationally, and internationally
- Use of buildings and grounds by the school community and outsiders
- Bids required for contracts for goods and services
- Financial management, especially checks and balances
- Investment management
- Admission
- Financial aid
- Gift acceptance
- Bonds for paid staff and volunteers who handle money
- Publications, videos, and electronic media that portray the school, especially its admission policy, programs, and facilities

APPENDIX F

Sample Board Member Job Description

The board of trustees supports the work of the school and provides mission-based leadership to ensure the school's health and welfare both now and in the future. Service on the board is for a _____ year term that is renewable. Responsibilities of individual trustees include the following:

- Making a commitment of time to the school, including attending all board and committee/task force meetings as required and fully reading all materials before board meetings.

- Understanding fully the roles and responsibilities of nonprofit governance, including respecting appropriate boundaries.

- Participating fully in board meetings and serving on at least one committee and/or task force.

- Volunteering for board assignments, particularly those that take advantage of the skills and expertise that he or she brings to the board.

- Being fully knowledgeable about the mission, vision, and strategic priorities of the school and making decisions that support them; staying informed on those trends, challenges, and/or opportunities that could affect the school.

- Participating fully in board self-assessments and professional development.

- Ensuring the ongoing financial health of the school by staying informed on the school's performance metrics and participating in the adoption of the school's annual budget and the review of the audit.

- Contributing to the head of school evaluation.

- Identifying and recruiting board members; making a commitment to building a diverse board.

- Giving to the school financially to the best of his or her ability and making the school a giving priority during time of board service.

- Serving as an ambassador for the school with all stakeholder groups and with the larger external community.
- Keeping all board deliberations and actions confidential.
- Participating in major school activities.
- Getting to know other board members and school personnel and building strong, respectful relationships.

APPENDIX G
Sample Trustee Commitment Letter

Dear Trustee,

As a member of the board of trustees, you are in a position to make a significant contribution to School X and its students. The vitality of the school depends on your commitment and imaginative and caring leadership. You and the other members of the board are trust holders of all that is important to the life of the school and, as such, need to be clear about your responsibilities.

I am asking each trustee to review and sign off on the following areas of personal commitment. These are your responsibilities as a member of the board of School X:

1. Attend board of trustees meetings held X times a year. Your presence is valued and your active participation is a critical component of board deliberations. Therefore, according to the bylaws, after three unexcused absences, it is assumed that you do not want to serve.

2. Serve on a minimum of one committee or task force. Much work of the board is accomplished through its committees, and your expertise will help move the board's agenda forward.

3. Read and be familiar with material sent to you in advance of board and committee meetings. Since we operate using a consent agenda model, we expect you to read materials relating to service on the board in a timely manner so that we can use board time for discussions on pressing topics, strategy sessions, or board education and growth, and not reports.

4. Support the school financially to the best of your ability. We expect 100 percent of the board to contribute to the annual fund and also to any capital or endowment campaigns. Your support tells other potential contributors that our board of trustees is tangibly committed as

donors. Trustees serve as key resources for access to other individuals, foundations, and corporations where they have influence.

5. Make decisions that are in the best interest of the school. We all wear many hats — for example, parent or alum of the school — but when making decisions, you may have to take that hat off so as not to be unduly influenced by the needs or wants of any one group. Your responsibility is to the long-term success of the school as a whole.

Just as you have responsibilities to the school, you also have the right to expect that the school will fulfill its responsibilities to you as a member of its board of trustees:

1. You can anticipate a judicious and respectful use of your time. The asset of time is one of the most vital resources busy people, such as you, have. We are committed to using your time in a manner that will return value to your personal contribution. If we fail in our attempt, please let me know.

2. We will get important information — including meeting agendas, minutes, financial reports, committee updates, and reports requiring action — to you in a timely manner before each meeting. We will also keep you informed about any critical events or concerns that may arise between meetings. Please let me know if the format of our reports does not facilitate your participation in the board's work. Are they too long, too terse, or confusing? Can you ask the important questions that need to be asked from the information provided?

3. We will provide you with a thorough orientation to the board and the school and ongoing training and education to help you be the most effective trustee you can be.

4. We will provide directors and officers liability insurance. If you were to be accused of wrongful acts committed while performing your trustee duties, you are indemnified against reasonable costs of defense proceedings, damages, judgments, and settlement costs up to $XX per occurrence. Wrongful acts covered include making errors in statements or mistaking information, making misleading statements or admissions, performing misleading acts, and neglecting or breaching duties

whether proven or accused. Willful negligence or criminal activity are not covered.

5. Please feel free to contact me at _____. I look forward to hearing from you, whether it is with questions or concerns on school and board issues or with praise of school and board accomplishments. The quality of School X depends upon a committed, knowledgeable, and involved board of trustees.

I look forward to serving with you and accomplishing results that will make a difference in the lives of our very special students. If you concur with these responsibilities, I would appreciate your signature of commitment. Please return one copy to me.

Sincerely,
Jane Doe
Chair of the Board

APPENDIX H
Board Profile Grid

Schools can create a grid or simply group board members by categories. The point is to get a visual representation of the board's profile.

NAME:											
Sex:											
Male											
Female											
Age:											
21–35											
36–50											
51–65											
Over 65											
Race/Ethnicity:											
African American											
American Indian/Alaskan Native											
Asian or Pacific Islander											
Caucasian											
Latina/o											
Other											

NAME:											
Profession:											
Arts											
Banking											
Business owner											
Civil service											
Corporate											
Education: Elementary											
Secondary											
Higher education											
Entrepreneur											
Finance											
Human relations											
Law											
Media											
Medicine											
Politics											
Religion											
Social services											

NAME:												
Area of Expertise:												
Administration — General												
Education												
Facilities management												
Financial management												
Fund-raising												
Health care												
Information services/technology												
Legal affairs												
Media/public relations												
Nonprofit governance												
Personnel management												
Strategic planning												
Constituency:												
Parent												
Past parent												
Grandparent												
Alumna/us												
Funder												
Community member												
Other												

NAME:												
Additional Characteristics:												
Ability to raise image												
Ability to raise students												
Ability to raise money												

The above items are only illustrative. A board profile grid needs to be customized for each school's specific needs. Sometimes it is most appropriate to select only those items that are truly crucial for the board when the evaluation is being undertaken.

APPENDIX I

Sample Goals for a Head of School

Program Related (Priority Goals)

- Manage a successful reaccreditation process

- Manage the process for faculty and staff growth and evaluation by completing and implementing the final components of the faculty evaluation system

- Conduct an assessment of current state of diversity work and aspirations from all school's constituencies

Financially Related (Priority Goals)

- Achieve budgeted enrollment

- Continue to work with the Financial Sustainability Task Force and make recommendations to the board for creating a more sustainable financial infrastructure for the school

- Cultivate and strengthen giving to the school, with particular emphasis on alumni and trustee giving; work to improve the overall strength of the development operation

- Create a timeline for the development of the next strategic plan, including a long-term budget addressing central issues of tuition, faculty compensation, meeting bank obligations, and financial aid

Communication Related

- In conjunction with the admissions director, create a unified marketing and communications plan to tell the school's story most effectively to prospective families

- Educate the board on less well understood parts of the program as indicated in the board assessment (e.g., organizational structure and responsibilities, hiring policies and procedures, risk management, accreditation, etc.)

APPENDIX J
Sample Job Description for a Head of School

Job Summary

As the chief executive officer of the school, the head of school pursues the vision and executes the stated mission of the school, manages faculty and staff, and ensures the financial health of the institution.

Essential Duties and Responsibilities

- Work in partnership with the board of trustees to manifest and refine the school's mission and strategic future; articulate that mission to all constituencies, including students, faculty and staff, parents, alumni/ae, and the broader community; and embody and represent the mission of the school with all constituencies.

- Carry out and review established school policies with the board of trustees; serve as a liaison to the board of trustees, keeping them informed on all aspects of the school's operation; represent the board to the faculty, staff, students, parents, and other constituencies.

- Provide leadership in shaping the school's programs (academic, athletic, and other extracurricular offerings).

- Have direct supervision over and responsibly provide direction to administration and faculty to ensure that school policies are followed.

- Be responsible for attracting, selecting, hiring, retaining, developing, and evaluating properly qualified faculty and staff, as well as terminating personnel when needed.

- Supervise the financial management, maintenance of the physical plant, strategic planning, and fund-raising efforts of the school.

- Maintain school culture and quality of life; provide a safe environment for learning.

- Ensure that every element of school life reflects the principles of equity, justice, and the dignity of each individual.
- Understand education trends and the local and regional education landscape.
- Communicate effectively with all constituencies, including students, faculty and staff, parents, and alumni/ae.
- Represent with integrity his or her role within the broader network of schools and the community.
- Abide by principles of good practice in all school operations — particularly admission, marketing, faculty recruitment, and fund-raising.

Other Duties

[Include any other duties that may be required of the position, such as coaching responsibilities, dorm duties, advising, or other specific duties. Be sure to include any job duties unique to the position, such as work hours, travel, evening and weekend duties, public appearances, etc.]

Common Qualification Requirements

- A bachelor's degree; master's or doctorate degree preferred
- Proven success in a senior administrative role
- Successful teaching experience and demonstrated leadership qualities
- Commitment to academic goals of students and the mission and philosophy of the school
- Excellent oral and written communication skills
- Emotional intelligence
- The ability to get along with coworkers and other school community members

APPENDIX K

Sample Board Meeting Agenda

I. **Call to Order** — A welcome from the chair, who also shares the objectives of the meeting and reviews the agenda.

II. **Consent Agenda*** — The items on this agenda are passed by consent (without a vote if there is no objection) or by formal vote. Single items can be taken off the agenda and considered separately if even only one member wishes to do so. Typical items on this agenda are minutes, routine ratification, and board approval required by the bylaws, such as the approval of banking relations. As a matter of risk management, never put the treasurer's report in a consent agenda because the figures have not been audited and the board does not want to be held legally accountable for what could be inaccurate numbers.

III. **Dashboard Review*** — An opportunity for the board to review key operating metrics like enrollment, budget performance, student/faculty attrition, etc., to ensure the ongoing health and well-being of the school. A treasurer's report also may be given at this time.

IV. **Head's Report*** — An opportunity for trustees to ask questions on the head's written report and for the head to share confidential items she or he did not want to put in writing. The head can also use this time to update trustees on broad educational issues and trends and/or progress toward goals.

V. **Committee/Task Force Reports*** — These begin with committees and task forces that have action items, followed by time for questions about other reports. Remember that committees and task forces do not need to be on every agenda if they have neither sent out a report nor proposed action items.

VI. **Issues Discussion/In-Depth Board Education*** — This area of the agenda should get 50 percent of the board's meeting time unless a committee or task force has major business to bring for a board decision during the report section above. Task forces can use this time to solicit input from trustees on the strategic issue they are examining. This is the part of the agenda where the board can break into smaller groups or have interactive education or training.

VII. Old (Unfinished) Business — Items that have been postponed or not finished at previous meetings.

VIII. New Business/Open Discussion — An opportunity for any trustee to bring up items that have not been placed on the agenda. However, it is not good practice for board members to bring up major issues at this time because there likely would not be time for a thorough discussion. This session also provides time to comment on trends, challenges, and opportunities trustees may have observed, some of which the board may follow up on at future meetings.

IX. Evaluation of the Meeting — Can be a two-minute quick appraisal. The board answers two questions: "What went well?" and "What did not?"

X. Adjournment

* Materials sent to trustees in advance of the board meeting.

APPENDIX L

Officer Qualifications Criteria

Board officers (the board chair, vice chair, treasurer, and secretary) should be:

- committed to the school's mission and vision and the goals of the strategic plan;
- willing to assume responsibility;
- able to exercise authority;
- skilled at team-building;
- able and willing to make decisions, especially in a collaborative decision-making setting;
- knowledgeable about the school;
- able to work well with the head;
- committed to continually updating governance knowledge and skills;
- able to see the big picture for the school;
- focused on strategic issues and able to help others focus on the same;
- sensitive to cliques and power struggles but disassociated from them;
- skilled at delegating responsibility to others;
- able to develop potential leaders;
- skilled at long-range strategic planning;
- able to problem-solve;
- effective oral and written communicators;
- familiar with parliamentary procedure and able to preside at meetings; and
- committed to raising funds for the school, making personal contributions, and setting an example for other trustees.

These attributes are not in priority order. It would be appropriate for a committee on trustees to set the priorities that apply to its school and to add qualities/qualifications that are uniquely important to the school.

APPENDIX M

Goals Action Plan Form

Goal What do we hope to achieve? (Make this outcome-based.)	
Performance Measure How will we know if we are successful? How will we measure progress along the way?	
Connection to Mission/Vision How does this goal support the school's mission or vision?	
Responsibility Which individual/committee/task force is responsible for leading this work?	
Target Date When do we expect to bring this work to fruition?	
Resources What funds, skills/abilities, research, and/or information do we need to accomplish this goal?	

APPENDIX N

Conflict-of-Interest Statement

This following sample policy has been generously provided by Ravenscroft School as an example of what schools may want to consider when drafting their own policies in this area. It is not, nor should it be relied upon as, legal advice. Neither Ravenscroft School nor NAIS warrants or guarantees the appropriateness of this or any other form for other independent schools. It is provided for general educational purposes only.

X SCHOOL CONFLICT-OF-INTEREST POLICY

ARTICLE I — PURPOSE

The purpose of the conflict-of-interest policy is to protect X School ("the school") and its interest when it is contemplating entering into a transaction or arrangement that might benefit the private interest of an officer, member of the board of trustees ("trustee"), or member of the administration of the school or that might result in a possible excess benefit transaction. This policy is intended to supplement but not replace any applicable state and federal laws governing conflict of interest applicable to nonprofit and charitable organizations or any provisions in the school's bylaws.

ARTICLE II — DEFINITIONS

A. **Interested Person:** Any trustee, officer, member of the administration, or member of a committee with governing board delegated powers who has a direct or indirect financial interest, as defined below, is an interested person. If a person is an interested person with respect to any affiliate of the organization, he or she is an interested person with respect to all affiliates.

B. **Financial Interest:** A person has a financial interest if the person has, directly or indirectly, through business, investment, or family:

1. an ownership or investment interest in any entity with which the school has a transaction or arrangement;

2. a compensation arrangement with the school or with any entity or individual with which the school has a transaction or arrangement; or

3. a potential ownership or investment interest in, or compensation arrangement with, any entity or individual with which the school is negotiating a transaction or arrangement. Compensation includes direct and indirect remuneration as well as gifts or favors that are not insubstantial.

A financial interest is not necessarily a conflict of interest. Under Article III, Section B, a person who has a financial interest may have a conflict of interest only if the appropriate governing board or committee decides that a conflict of interest exists.

ARTICLE III — PROCEDURES

A. **Duty to Disclose:** In connection with any actual or possible conflict of interest, an interested person must disclose the existence of the financial interest and be given the opportunity to disclose all material facts to the trustees and members of committees with governing board delegated powers or others considering the proposed transaction or arrangement.

B. **Determining Whether a Conflict of Interest Exists:** After disclosure of the financial interest and all material facts, and after any discussion with the interested person, he or she shall leave the governing board or committee meeting while the determination of a conflict of interest is discussed and voted upon. The remaining board or committee members shall decide whether a conflict of interest exists.

C. **Procedures for Addressing the Conflict of Interest:**

1. An interested person may make a presentation at the governing board or committee meeting, but after the presentation, he or

she shall leave the meeting during the discussion of, and the vote on, the transaction or arrangement involving the possible conflict of interest.

2. The chairperson of the governing board or committee shall, If appropriate, appoint a disinterested person or committee to investigate alternatives to the proposed transaction or arrangement.

3. After exercising due diligence, the governing board or committee shall determine whether the school can obtain with reasonable efforts a more advantageous transaction or arrangement from a person or entity that would not give rise to a conflict of interest.

4. If a more advantageous transaction or arrangement is not reasonably possible under circumstances not producing a conflict of interest, the governing board or committee shall determine by a majority vote of the disinterested trustees whether the transaction or arrangement is in the school's best interest, for its own benefit, and whether it is fair and reasonable. In conformity with the above determination, it shall make its decision as to whether to enter into the transaction or arrangement.

D. **Violations of the Conflict-of-Interest Policy:**

1. If the governing board or committee has reasonable cause to believe a member has failed to disclose actual or possible conflicts of interest, it shall inform the member of the basis for such belief and afford the member an opportunity to explain the alleged failure to disclose.

2. If, after hearing the member's response and after making further investigation as warranted by the circumstances, the governing board or committee determines that the member has failed to disclose an actual or possible conflict of interest, it shall take appropriate disciplinary and corrective action.

ARTICLE IV — RECORDS OF PROCEEDINGS

The minutes of the board and all committees with board-delegated powers shall contain:

A. the names of the persons who disclosed or otherwise were found to have a financial interest in connection with an actual or possible conflict of interest, the nature of the financial interest, any action taken to determine whether a conflict of interest was present, and the governing board's or committee's decision as to whether a conflict of interest in fact existed; and

B. the names of the persons who were present for discussions and votes relating to the transaction or arrangement; the content of the discussion, including any alternatives to the proposed transaction or arrangement; and a record of any votes taken in connection with the proceedings.

ARTICLE V — COMPENSATION

A voting member of the governing board who receives compensation, directly or indirectly, from the school for services is precluded from voting on matters pertaining to that member's compensation.

A. A voting member of any committee whose jurisdiction includes compensation matters and who receives compensation, directly or indirectly, from the school for services is precluded from voting on matters pertaining to that member's compensation.

B. No voting member of the governing board or any committee whose jurisdiction includes compensation matters and who receives compensation, directly or indirectly, from the school, either individually or collectively, is prohibited from providing information to any committee regarding compensation.

ARTICLE VI — ANNUAL STATEMENTS

Each trustee, officer and member of a committee with governing board delegated powers, and member of the administration (as applicable) shall annually sign a statement that affirms that such person:

A. has received a copy of the conflict-of-interest policy;

B. has read and understands the policy;

C. has agreed to comply with the policy; and

D. understands that the school is charitable and in order to maintain its federal tax exemption it must engage primarily in activities that accomplish one or more of its tax-exempt purposes.

ARTICLE VII — PERIODIC REVIEWS

To ensure that the school operates in a manner consistent with charitable purposes and does not engage in activities that could jeopardize its tax-exempt status, periodic reviews shall be conducted. The periodic reviews shall, at a minimum, include the following subjects:

A. Whether compensation arrangements and benefits are reasonable, based on competent survey information, and the result of arm's-length bargaining

B. Whether partnerships, joint ventures, and arrangements with management organizations conform to the school's written policies, are properly recorded, reflect reasonable investment or payments for goods and services, further charitable purposes, and do not result in inurement, impermissible private benefit, or in an excess benefit transaction

ARTICLE VIII — USE OF OUTSIDE EXPERTS

When conducting the periodic reviews as provided for in Article VII, the school may, but need not, use outside advisors. If outside experts are used, their use shall not relieve the governing board of its responsibility for ensuring that periodic reviews are conducted.

ARTICLE IX — FURTHER POLICIES

The school shall adopt further conflict-of-interest policies applicable to the administration, faculty, and staff of the school.

About the Authors

Donna Orem is the chief operating officer at the National Association of Independent Schools (NAIS). She directs the organization's strategic planning process, manages the day-to-day work of the office, and oversees human resources and staff development. Orem has served as a trustee for several organizations, including service as the chair of one independent school board and vice chair of another.

Debra P. Wilson is general counsel at NAIS. She monitors and analyzes regulatory and legal issues relevant to all aspects of independent schools. She develops legal advisories for independent schools and amicus briefs for key court cases and acts as counsel for NAIS. She has served on the boards of two independent schools, including service as board chair for one of those boards.